Dan Bradbury

BREEDING
GAZELLES

FAST GROWTH STRATEGIES
FOR YOUR BUSINESS

Editing and Project Management: Karen Rowe
Cover Design: Moyez Khan
Interior Design: Ljiljana Pavkov

Printed in the United Kingdom
ISBN: 978-0-9954532-0-3

Published by Chiddingstone Publishing

"Dan is like my new iPhone. I look at him at least 200 times a day…he annoys the f#%k out of me, and I feel like throwing him at a wall most days…he often doesn't do what I want him to…and is too awkward to walk around with in my pocket…BUT - he's also really useful, ultimately makes my life better, looks quite sexy and I like the way he feels in my hand!"

— *James Lavers*, *founder of The Lazy Coach,*
Entrepreneur and Speaker

"I first met Dan in 2007 and I'm as impressed today as I was back then at his extensive knowledge & proven experience in business success, coaching, direct response marketing, and online/digital marketing. Listen and do what he says - it will serve you well."

— *Dave Lee*, *Co-Founder, SixthDivision & PlusThis*

"I first met Dan when he approached me out of the blue, offering to optimise an aspect of my business. He said he didn't want anything in return; that he just wanted to see if he could make a difference. I said yes, he did what he said he would, and we've been friends ever since. In a world full of people looking for what they can get, Dan deeply understands how to lead by giving, serving and over-delivering. It's been a huge pleasure to see Dan going from strength to strength as an entrepreneur and a businessman, and I'm fascinated to see what he builds next."

— *Jamie Smart*, *#1 Bestselling Author,*
Educator and Entrepreneur

Dan Bradbury is one of the good guys - smart, loyal and supportive. His belief in me helped see me through one of the toughest, but also best years I've had in business. There's a lot of ego and scarcity mentality in this industry, so when you find someone who has an abundant mentality, it renews your faith. Dan didn't just believe in me, he actually put himself out to actively help me… and continues to do so. Glad to call him my friend.'

– *Shaa Wasmund MBE*, *Best Selling Author,*
Entrepreneur and Speaker

"I've watched Dan grow from strength to strength over the last decade…what's incredible are his high standards and his pursuit of excellence. He is rapidly becoming the go to guy - to understand and implement the latest strategies and systems to take your business from ordinary to extraordinary. He's special and rare and a decent guy with high integrity - he's also someone I'm proud to have as a friend"

— *Greg Secker*, *CEO of Knowledge to Action*
and International Speaker

"I've had the pleasure of growing as an entrepreneur and business owner over the last 10 years with Dan Bradbury. In many ways, we've grown up on the journey together. He's the only person I've ever lost an award to, and he earned it. Having grown my company NPE now to over $10M in annual revenues and listed 6x on the Inc 500/5000 list in the USA, there are many experts and thought leaders we call upon when working on major initiatives. But Dan is someone who we routinely engage with for his great experience and insights when it comes to sales and marketing strategy. He gets it and loves to cut through the clutter as much as we do to get to the goal. If you're looking to grow your company to the next level, Dan is someone I highly recommend you speak with. He brings a tremendous amount of passion and leadership to the table."

— **Sean Greeley**, *CEO NPE*

"There are fewer than a handful of people in the world I would trust to take control of my business and Dan is on that shortlist. His business-savvy wisdom goes way beyond his years."

— **Topher Morrison**, *Managing Director,
Key Person of Influence USA*

"Dan's commitment to excellence and to helping others achieve excellence is astounding. He helped me to Realise the #1 missing link in my business and I have since taken action to get this resolved. In the two months since we met, I have seen a 4x increase in my productivity and in my bottom line."

— **Karen Rowe**, *#1 International bestselling author,
CEO Front Rowe Seat Communications*

Table of Contents

To my three children:

Summer, Jenson, and India,
who showed me the real meaning
and purpose of life.

"Every morning in Africa, a gazelle wakes up, it knows it must outrun the fastest lion or it will be killed. Every morning in Africa, a lion wakes up. It knows it must run faster than the slowest gazelle, or it will starve. It doesn't matter whether you're the lion or a gazelle — when the sun comes up, you'd better be running."

— CHRISTOPHER MCDOUGALL, AUTHOR

ACKNOWLEDGMENTS

The biggest inspiration for this book is my mentor, Keith J. Cunningham, whose business knowledge and wisdom helped me to start, build, and exit my own Gazelle company.

To Jay Abraham, who taught me that anything is possible with just a little creative genius.

I want to acknowledge Daniel Priestley for leading the way in my work with Gazelles.

To Steve Bolton, my fellow autodidact polymath, thank you for showing me the magic of thinking big.

To Chris Matthews, for helping me to kick the can, every single day.

To Jeremy Harbour, the smartest guy I know on the topic of selling companies.

To Clate Mask and Scott Martineau, founders of Infusionsoft, for showing me the power of vision and culture to build a lasting legacy.

I want to thank Topher Morrison, my longstanding friend, for finally getting me to write this book.

And to Emma Garcia, the world's best personal assistant, without you, my life would be a mess.

PREFACE

What you are about to read has transformed my life, and it might just do the same for you, too.

Just a few short years ago by most people's standards I was "successful". I had a mid six-figure business, I had a small team of hard working employees, I had a nice house, a nice car and a good income.

But I was exceptionally frustrated. I felt like I had hit an invisible ceiling. Because no matter what I did I just couldn't seem to break through. Sales would increase for a month or two, then come right back down again. Despite doing the right things, cash flow always seemed tight. The end of the month was often a squeeze with me not taking my salary to make sure I made payroll.

And then something changed.

I applied the strategies you will find in this book and things took off. Rapidly.

It was a bit like being on a rocketship at times, the sheer speed of change was enough to take your breath away. We had to change offices, twice in an eighteen-month period because we outgrew the space we were in. We were recruiting and training multiple new team members every single month. Our revenue increased by almost 100% per year, for three years in a row.

And it wasn't just me. At first, I shared the information from this book with just a handful of friends and clients. The results were dramatic; you'll read about some of them in this book. There were revenue increases from £250k to £500k on the low end, to one client who increased from £8 million to almost £26 million on the high end!

But be warned, being a fast growing gazelle company isn't easy. Having now taught this material to over 8,000 different business owners from over 69 different countries around the world, I know what works. To become a gazelle company requires an entirely different mindset, as well as specific skills and tools. This book provides you with both.

To paraphrase Einstein, the level of thinking that got you to the level you are at today will not get you to the level you want to get to. In actual fact, it inhibits it. (Read on for proof!)

Many of the ideas in this book will challenge you. Some may even directly oppose what you believe to be true. But after my 9+ years breeding gazelle companies all I can say is the strategies in this book are tried and tested. I strongly encourage you to study them carefully, put them into action and judge the results for yourself.

Now, get a cup of coffee, roll up your sleeves and let's get to work!

WHAT IS A GAZELLE?

"Turnover is vanity, profit is sanity but cash flow is king."

— UNKNOWN

A question: Would you rather have a ten million pound company with no profit, or a two million pound company with half a million of net profit?

The choice is obvious, right?

Maybe not.

Clients come to me all the time, seeking to grow their revenue, and if these conversations have taught me one thing it's that people tend to fall into two categories. The first group tells me they would rather make the net profit but, from an emotional standpoint, it is obvious they dream of having the revenue. The second group clearly chose the ten million pound company with no profit.

Why on earth would they choose to break even over having half a million pounds worth of profit?

Well, because they believe that, when they have a bigger and better company, *then* they will be able to figure out how to make it profitable. This is never the case, however.

At ten million, a company has that much more risk and vulnerability. That level of risk does not need to be dangerous… not if you understand how to achieve disciplined growth and build your company in a sustainable way. That is to say, not if you choose to be a gazelle.

You may raise an eyebrow. Gazelle? Like the animal known for running swiftly across the Savannah? Well, no. The gazelle I'm talking about is the lifeblood of the economy.

The first person to use the term "gazelle" in the context of business was David L. Birch when he was a researcher at the Massachusetts Institute of Technology. According to Inc. magazine, Birch was looking for "a simple, almost naïve way of explaining what was going on in the economy." Looking to the natural world for inspiration, Birch created a way of categorising business by using elephants, mice, and gazelles to explain the principles he was observing. "The big companies, elephants, are slow and not very innovative," he said. "Then there are a large number of very small firms, mice, that run around but fail to develop. And then the gazelles…small firms that grow quickly and create employment." By Birch's reasoning, a gazelle is a company that, not unlike its real life counterpart, can "run fast and jump high." The term caught on and soon became part of business lexicon.

But gazelles don't just grow fast. They grow consistently, with creativity and innovation. A gazelle is any fast-growing company with over one million in revenue that increases its profits by at least 20% annually for four years or more. Over that four year period, a gazelle grows so much that their greatest growth point is always found at the end of four years. Using this criteria, only about one in every 16 companies with employees qualifies. It is the pace of this rapid growth, rather than their size, that allows not only small companies but very large enterprises to be considered gazelles. Clearly, when it comes to success in the business world, it pays to be a gazelle.

It has been commonly believed, for most of this century, that new jobs are almost entirely created by big companies. In the late 1970s, however, Birch discovered that nearly all net job growth was in fact created by a small percentage of companies. Initially, some 82 percent of the gazelles had fewer than 19 employees, while just 3.6 percent had 100 or more. That contingent of larger companies proved to be "superstars," generating 53 percent of the net new jobs created by the entire group during the five years studied. Some of the superstars were already Fortune 500 companies in 1990. Others would join that list later.

These findings turned Birch's earlier conclusions upside down, saying, in effect, that size didn't matter. Although most gazelles were small companies, only a tiny percentage of small companies were gazelles, and the most prolific job-creators among them weren't particularly small at all.

You're probably thinking that, since that research in 1990, we know a great deal more about creating a business environment conducive to the growth and proliferation of gazelles. But we don't.

We don't know why one company becomes a gazelle and another doesn't, or why some gazelles keep creating jobs while others stop. Nor do we know the growth-impeding obstacles common to gazelles. Most troubling of all, we don't know why the percentage of growing companies has fallen over the last ten years. And we're just beginning to learn what new government policies could improve the situation—and what current policies are making matters worse. Indeed, as Verne Harnish, founder of the worldwide Entrepreneurs Organisation, noted, gazelle companies have the potential to drive economic recovery, although they have yet to receive the support required to thrive.

Of course, having experience with a gazelle of my own, I do have some ideas about the process. From what I have observed, most companies fail to become gazelles because the business approach that brought them to one level is what prevents them from getting to the next. For example, a business can reach 100k in revenue because the owner hustles and is good at what he does. Unfortunately, a company will not be able to grow to seven figures with an owner doing everything himself. Owners must learn to delegate, and build growth into the business model. Additionally, the bigger a company gets, the harder it is to find successful models to copy and learn from – models of gazelles, not elephants or mice.

This is why I say gazelles are the lifeblood of the economy, specifically because of the way they disrupt archaic, established industries. Take crowd funding platforms, companies like The Funding Circle and Zopa, which are interfering with the big banks' monopoly on lending. These are excellent examples of fast-growing gazelles that have created many new jobs, while giving their customers better service.

Given that potential for success, I now work specifically with gazelles, all of whom are run by creative business owners solving meaningful problems that are changing the world. It requires innovation to solve these problems, but when a great solution comes to market, everyone benefits. The world benefits.

That said, we can't reap the benefits unless the ideas get out there. This means the business end of the process needs to work. I want to help the world, and I do so by helping people with good ideas develop the business skills to take those ideas to market, get funding, and realise their vision.

The vast majority of small businesses fail: 40 percent in the first year, 80 percent in five years, and 94 percent in 10 years. Of the remaining six percent, less than ten percent of those get over $1 million in annual revenue. Gazelles account for 80 percent of new jobs created by small companies. If you can get over the hurdles inherent in going from a small business to a fast growing company, you can leapfrog from half a million to ten-million-plus in revenue and create a business that you've always desired.

Though clearly the ideal, being a gazelle is dangerous because fast growth inherently involves great risk. The level of thinking that got you to your first half a million in revenue will not get you to ten million. To enter the world of gazelles requires a paradigm shift that reaches beyond your mind and into your business model.

And that is what this book is about.

In Part One, I will show you the key principles necessary to observe and analyse your business. Part Two will guide you in designing your own business strategy and creating the business plan to generate your desired results. In Part Three, we tackle execution. Remember, you can have the world's best strategy but, unless executed effectively, it's never going to work.

Gazelles are created by innovators and leaders with vision. As such, I have conducted interviews with key leaders in their industries, Jay Abraham, Ryan Deiss, Daniel Priestley, Sean Greeley, Rob Moore and Steve Bolton. Learn from some of the greats about the greatest challenges they experienced, most valuable lessons learned along the way, and benefit from their best advice and secrets for scaling your business. Throughout this book, it is my desire to show you the practical tools you need to turn your idea into a gazelle, a company that not only provides a product but is inherently designed for rapid and sustainable growth. Companies that create jobs leave legacies. Will yours be one of them?

CHAPTER 1

YOU HAVE NO IDEA WHAT YOU ARE DOING

"Only when the tide goes out do you discover who's been swimming naked."

— WARREN BUFFETT

"We did a lot of things right, we got up to £40 or £50 million a year in revenue. But we made the mistake of thinking we knew what we were doing."

Richard Reed, Co-founder of Innocent Smoothies, a juice company he sold to Coca-Cola for over £100 million in cash, spoke at one of my recent events.

"We just got lucky, he says. "For ten years of the business, we had no major problems. Then the recession hit, and we were within hours of going out of business because of a few stupid mistakes."

According to Bill Gates, "Success is a lousy teacher. It seduces smart people into thinking they can't lose." Richard admits the company got lazy due to past success and made some critical mistakes - like only having one supplier who manufactured his smoothies, so when that supplier went bust, it nearly ruined the whole business. Or when they signed a bank loan with very stiff penalties if growth didn't occur at a certain rate. When they didn't reach that rate of growth due to the financial crisis, the bank very nearly called in the loan. That would have ended the business.

"The game never ends; there are always going to be big problems," Richard stresses. "Your job as a business owner or entrepreneur is to make sure that you're not making the same mistakes and having the same problems over and over again. Make them bigger, higher quality problems."

If you've picked up this book, you must be ready to stop lying. You must be ready to admit that you have no clue what you're doing. I know you think you do, but you're not telling yourself the truth. You've just gotten lucky.

You're a smart person, you've worked hard, you've got some traction, and you're able to sell some stuff, but in reality, you are a slave to your business.

You are lying to yourself and everyone around you. Your business is on life support.

Likely you have set goals for yourself and your business in the past. Goal setting is not where it's at.

Goals are the effect, not the cause.

The goal setting, the visualisation, is the exciting bit. It's important to define your end point initially, but most people spend so much time focused on the end outcome, they forget they have got to actually MOVE!

Pretty much everybody on the planet wants to be fitter, sexier, richer, but wanting it does not make it happen.

Most people have the goal, but in reality, very few are prepared to do what it takes to make it happen. They are lying to themselves, saying they 'want it'. They don't.

I believe, if we spend the majority of our time focused on the daily disciplines, the critical drivers that, if consistently done, will produce the effects that we want, we would all make much more progress towards our goals.

Most business owners live in a fantasyland. Whenever they talk about the future, there are always big plans, goals and ideals. Big dreams that are "almost there" or "just around the corner." But as soon as you ask about the previous twelve months, there's an immediate change of heart, a justification as to why they didn't hit their goals.

An excuse.

They are looking for a big win, the thing that will finally make this business work, overcome all past losses, a sudden breakthrough to a new level of profits and opportunity… and it's complete and utter bollocks. It just doesn't happen that way.

Not in the real world. And when it appears to, what you are actually observing is the "compound effect."

What is the compound effect? Einstein described it as the eighth wonder of the world.

Keith J. Cunningham would describe it as "ordinary things, consistently done, producing extraordinary results." One of the best books I've read on this subject is *The Compound Effect* by Darren Hardy. In it, Darren explains how, if you are constantly making incremental improvements, at first it feels like nothing is happening, but if you persist, then you gain huge momentum.

If you take one penny and double it every day for thirty-one days (so it's two pennies on day two, four pennies on day three, etc.), how much money would you have on the last day?

Over £10.7 million!

However, on day sixteen, you're over halfway there and yet all you'd have is £327.68—do the math and see for yourself. And that's why most business owners give up. They feel like they are putting in all this effort and not getting rewarded. Or worse, they get impatient and take a stupid risk that sets them back years, just before they were about to get the 'overnight success' they'd been looking for.

Massive leverage can and does happen, but the little wins need to be gained first.

There's no specific requirement that you must slave for a certain period of time in business before you prosper, but you must keep consistently making incremental progress. Most people don't have the discipline to do this, and that's why they join the ranks of the majority of the population, who are just one month's paycheck away from oblivion.

Just a tiny two percent improvement in your income each month would see your pay increase by more than ten times in less than ten years. So dream big, by all means. Just make sure that, every single month, you're using the strategies, tactics, and case studies detailed in this book in order to get compounded results.

You're Stalled

You've hit a plateau. It's gotten harder to scale. The thinking that got you to your current level not what will get you to the next one. In fact, the thought process that got you where you are now is the very thing that will inhibit and prevent you from reaching that next level.

Different stages of business size and scale require different skillsets. The first stage is about taking massive action to get traction, throwing ideas up against the wall and seeing what sticks.

Your business was an infant, so it needed nurturing and hand-holding. It needed everything you were doing for it. But now, as you look to go from mid-six figures to seven figures, you have to have leverage, and leverage only comes in two forms: people and systems. In order to have a business that is self-sufficient, what Dan Sullivan, Founder of Strategic Coach, would call a self-managing company, that can live, breathe, exist and make money by itself, you need to have systems, processes, and people driving that business.

Unless you know how to set up the systems, and unless you know how to choose the right people, get those people on the bus, then manage and lead them, it's going to be your Achilles heel. It *will* be the weak link that snaps the chain.

You cannot get the scale that you want with the skills that brought you to this level. To go from mid-six to seven figures, and definitely to go from seven figures to eight figures, you need a different skillset. You need the skills contained in this book. Otherwise, you will be permanently stuck, working your ass off, taking less money home than your team members in some months while carrying all the stress, all the hassle, and all the risk. You're not getting return on investment.

You've managed to do the hard work, managed to get enough momentum to keep the business alive. And actually, it's not such a big shift to a radically transformative level of profitability, a hugely more profitable business. There are just a few little shifts, but you need to know what those shifts are. You need the information in this book

Most business owners are deluding themselves. Modest success makes you falsely believe you know what you are doing, but the reality is you don't have a clue. My biggest challenge is dealing with business owners who think, firstly, that they know what the problem is, and secondly, that they know the answers. They are mistaken. Like you, they know the answers that got them to this stage. Like you, they don't know the answers that will get them to the next level.

My biggest problem is dealing with business owners who think, firstly, that they know what the problem is, and secondly, that they know the answers.

Worse yet, at this point, you are lying to yourself and to everyone around you. Your past success means you get protective and try to defend your business systems. You don't want to lose the income streams coming to you, and you don't want to take on risk when you are finally starting to make a little bit of money.

Actually, you need to get real. In order to fix the problem, you need to first acknowledge that one exists. And the fact is, you don't have your act together.

In many respects, you just got lucky.

You are hanging on by the skin of your teeth, and problems are popping up. Fires flare up at different times, and your whole attention goes to them. Your business enslaves you, your phone never leaves your side, and you're always on, 24-7, 365.

It makes your spouse crazy that you're not available because the business is on life support. It's not about to die, but it's sick, and it all feels so unfair. You're trying to train somebody with a nagging knee injury to be an elite athlete. It doesn't make sense. You cannot have peak performance when, fundamentally, you have injuries and flaws.

Those flaws in your business will prevent you from ever being an elite athlete, ever increasing from a half million to ten million pounds. You need to address those issues. But first, you need to acknowledge you don't know it all. Then, rather than seeing some great idea on the internet and assuming that Facebook advertising will magically save the day, you need to learn how to look for the problems plaguing your business.

Staying Ahead of the Curve

In today's business world, you can't stay still. You need to continually improve, even just to stay still, and if you don't stay ahead of the radically moving marketplace, your business will be over.

Capitalism is the ultimate definition of survival of the fittest, and if you're not on the cutting edge of technology, if you're not well-versed in new skillsets, new business models, the latest economic trends, you're screwed. The business will be done and you will fail. It's important to remember that the accelerated pace of change is both the biggest threat *and* the biggest opportunity.

If you can stay ahead of the curve, not just react but correctly anticipate the right move, you, as Wayne Gretzky said, "can skate to where the puck is going", and you can reap rewards beyond your wildest imagination. It's not about getting lucky.

It's not about coming up with an idea to rival Uber. It's about identifying how you think about your business, how you approach your business, and how you make sure you stay ahead of the curve every single day, making the incremental changes necessary for maximum impact on your profitability.

It's never been a better time to be a small business owner. The trend, as we've come out of the last great recession, is increasingly pro small business. It's increasingly technology-led, which means more and more generic jobs being lost and more and more people being self-employed. This new technology means people can create new ideas, products, and services quickly, leading to great opportunity, as well as more competition than ever. There has never been a lower barrier to entry but, unless you have a competitive advantage, it will become harder and harder to make money.

The return on investment you seek can only be gained by having a competitive advantage, and that competitive advantage comes from having the skills and tools to outthink and outsmart the competition. One in a thousand people might get lucky. The only way to consistently give yourself a competitive advantage is to have the right system, the right process, which allows you to correctly analyse what's going on and make the best possible investments of your time and money.

This book will help you do three things:

1. Clarify a much bigger vision for your business. Your business is capable of so much more than you currently think. I will show you how to tap into that vision.

2. Correctly analyse the business to get the low hanging fruit. Knowing which screws to turn and which dials to move can have an exponential increase on your profitability. You'll learn to identify the easiest change you can

make to create the biggest impact and maximise the return on investment.

3. Leverage people so that your company is less dependent on you. Once it can exist as self-managing, meaning the right people and systems are in place, you can make the profit you deserve and have the time to enjoy it.

Most business owners can't see the wood for the trees. They're too wrapped up in all of the drama in their business. This book will help you identify the low hanging fruit. From reading this book, you will immediately identify something you can put in place that, within the next thirty days, will result in a notable difference in your bottom line profits and cash in your bank account.

Are You One Of the Top Two Percent?

The speed of change is also accelerating, however. And for those who don't stay on top of things, that means more businesses failing. The small business failure rate is going up, not down. Forty percent of businesses fail in the first year, over 80 percent within five years, and 94 percent within ten years. That's staggering, and of the remaining six percent, 90 percent of those won't get in excess of £1 million in revenue. *Revenue*. We're not even talking about profit, we're talking about revenue.

What that means to you, in plain English, is the business market has never been more competitive. It has never been easier for every man and his dog to get entry to the business marketplace. They all say that they want to get rich. In reality, that's fake ambition.

You ask any small business owner—ask as many as you can—they're all going to tell you that they want to get big, they want to make money, they want to have more free time, they want to change the world. But the reality is this: Most people are not willing to pay the price to get the results they want. They want to lose weight, but they're not prepared to exercise and watch their diet. Most small business owners are not willing to pay the price and learn the skills and tools they need to become a business master. They are not willing to do the work to be profitable in any industry, in any economic cycle, in any society, anywhere in the world.

Look At Things Differently

Einstein said insanity is doing the same thing over and over and expecting a different result. Yet, that's exactly what most business owners do. They are smoking, what I like to call, hopium. They are trying to do it a little bit better this year, hoping that, magically, it's going to work and they're going to make loads of money. Insanity indeed.

Instead, they need to look at things differently. They need a new skillset for the next level. They, and you, need a different way of thinking about business, of analysing business, of identifying opportunities and leveraging them just as you analyse and mitigate risks.

You need this new approach, this new way of thinking, this new set of tools to give you the cutting edge in the marketplace. This isn't about some gimmicky tactic of social media advertising. This isn't about some new doohickey that will be a fleeting fad. This is about a more elevated level of thinking, which gives you a better scope, a better view of how the world of business is working today and how to add value and maximise the profit potential therein.

There are countless so-called business gurus out there waiting to sell you their magic push-button solution. In reality, a lot of that is *bull*, and even those with good ideas still aren't good models for success.

To truly succeed, you must be masterful in a variety of different areas. You need to know marketing, you need to know sales, you need to know how to recruit the best people, how to manage the best people, how to provide strong customer service, and how to maintain great product development. You need to be able to do all of that simultaneously, which is where a lot of people run into trouble. Many of them have big dreams and ideas, but they aren't prepared to execute. They're not disciplined enough to put the right skills and tools to use, and to follow through consistently, day in and day out.

Great wealth isn't built overnight. If you believe that's possible, save your time and put this book away. This book is for serious business owners committed to mastering their craft, elevating their thinking and their skillsets to the next level, and reaping the long term rewards.

In the new economy, the losers are people who can't stay ahead of the curve, those who can't anticipate the changes and, when change happens, they get wiped out. The winners are the ones who learn and adapt the fastest, those who can think the clearest. They're the ones who quickly assess the situation and calibrate a new strategy to add value in the rapidly changing economy.

Throughout the book, I have incorporated interviews conducted with a number of these winners, these quick learners and fast adapters who have succeeded in becoming gazelles and even moving beyond gazelle status. I think it's important for you to hear, directly from their mouths, about their struggles, failures, realisations, and ultimate successes.

Interview with Ryan Deiss

My first such interview is with CEO Ryan Deiss, co-founder of Digital Marketer and executive chairman of nativecommerce.com, an e-commerce and digital media company. Ryan has a number of digital media and e-commerce companies like makeuptutorials.com, survivallife.com and sells a number of physical products, including menswear, accessories, and make-up products. His companies handle many different types of products and media sites. Then they take all the cool stuff they learn doing digital marketing – for both digital companies and bricks-and-mortar businesses – and systemise it and then report on it in Digital Marketer.

Dan: Like so many in the UK, it seems like your rise has been prolific. Tell us, how did you become a gazelle? What started or caused this fast growth?

Ryan: I started this company when I was a freshman at university in need of extra money. The internet was brand new at that time — I figured starting an online business seemed like a good way to get started because the start-up costs were low. I didn't really treat it as a business. I just treated it as an extra way to make money.

As a result, it was almost like a hobby, and I made a little bit of money when I did it. When I decided to treat it like a business, this little hobby was generating six figures a year in revenue, which became a significant little side project. I still went to get a job because I didn't think it was real business.

After working that job for six months, I realised I hated it and I needed to focus on the business. When I made the decision not to just have a business, but have a *company*, that was when my mindset shifted. This wasn't just a side project, it was a company, and I needed help.

At that time, I was frustrated because I realised I hadn't even checked the mail in over a month. I hadn't paid bills in a long time. It wasn't that I didn't have the money; I just didn't have the time. That was when I said, "Okay, if this is going to be a company, then there should be people around me."

The decision to make my very first hire propelled me from the quarter to half a million profit range up to seven figures. That one hire was what did it. That one hire took all the busy work off my plate so I could just focus on the high-value things, and that made all the difference. This administrative assistant checked the mail for me and did the basic things, the stuff that just clutters in my mind. That's been the lesson at every single time when we've been stuck.

Dan: *That's not uncommon.*

Ryan: We always had products. If you're going to be a successful business, you have to have a great product. That goes without saying. You have to deliver a phenomenal experience, and you have to be good at sales and marketing. If you don't have a great product and you're good at sales and marketing, then you'll quickly convince the world that you're terrible at what you do, and, if you have a bad product and you're bad at sales and marketing, at least your company with die a slower death.

Finally, if you have a great product and you're terrible at sales and marketing, growth is going to be difficult unless your product is truly extraordinary. These are what Peter Thiel calls a 10x type of product, things that are so much better, so different, and don't come along every day. So much money can be made just fulfilling people's basic needs, not necessarily creating the next Facebook, Uber, or Snapchat.

So let's assume you have a great product. Let's assume that you're great at sales and marketing. If we're talking about scaling, we're talking about becoming a gazelle and beyond, and it really does come down to people and systems.

Dan: *On the way, what were your biggest failures? What are some of the biggest lessons to come from growing a start-up six-figure company to seven or eight figures and beyond?*

Ryan: Yes, we're tracking to nine figures this year, so that's exciting. First of all, managing cash flow is, in many cases, more important than managing profit. Understanding the difference between the two was critical to me. Because there were times when I was thinking we were very, very profitable, but we had no money in the bank. I was buying advertising, and I understood what a customer was worth to me, but it wasn't worth that amount for 90 or 120 days.

So you hear a lot of people talk about LTV – lifetime customer value – and being able to buy at some amount less than that. I know it's common, for example, for SaaS companies here in the States. An acceptable acquisition to LTV is three to one. If they know the LTV is three, they'll spend one, so they're happy to acquire at a third of what the lifetime value is. But if you don't experience that lifetime value for two or three years, you can run out of cash while you're building a great business.

Understanding cash flow management was critical, simple things like setting aside enough money for taxes. When I was first getting started, I was buying a lot of advertising – buying,

buying, buying, buying, buying — and I racked up an enormous amount of debt. I thought it was okay to do it because I knew it would pay off one day. Well, my calculations were off. Before I knew it, I was a quarter-million dollars in debt, and I was kind of stuck.

That was the first time I messed up. I was able to dig myself out of the hole by deciding to stop spending money, to 'flee the margin.' Because it was still a good business, right? I've watched lots of good businesses blow up. So I had a good business, I had a product that people wanted, I was good at sales and marketing. I just had to stop spending money faster than I was making it.

And so I did. I paid attention to the flee the margin effect, which meant just doing what I had to do right now. Growth slowed down, but that was okay because our cash was going up. Sometimes you have to be okay with slower growth, unless you're, like the three to one SaaS companies. They can get away with that because they raise tens of millions, and in some cases, hundreds of millions of dollars.

Dan: *I don't think most business owners do know the difference between profit and cash flow. One of the biggest mistakes I see with companies that try to grow fast is that growth consumes cash by its very nature. So, the faster you're growing, the more you need to be in control of your cash flow.*

Ryan: The faster your business is growing, the faster your sales are growing. I've brought companies to the brink of utter collapse and failure because of growth, because of sales. It happens all the time. So cash flow management is crucial – watching your debt, making sure that you're not growing yourself into oblivion, and also setting funds aside for things like taxes.

When I finally got out of that hole I created with advertising debt, it did eventually pay off. It took a lot longer than I thought it would, but it was definitely worth it. I had to slow the growth for the second half of that year, hold off on investments, and just accumulate cash to pay off the debt. I sat there, breathing a deep sigh of relief. But the whole time I was doing that, I wasn't setting aside money for taxes.

I don't care where you live, you have to pay taxes. So now, after all this has happened, I go through the next year and find out I owe a quarter-million dollars in taxes to the government. So those two years, because I actually lost three years of growth, we were flat because I couldn't afford to grow. I used up all my cash by not managing it properly.

It's important to understand things like expense ratios – what percentage of your total sales are going to be made up by your people cost? If it's more than twenty percent, that can be a little scary, unless those people are also producing a bunch of your product, the cost of goods sold. If your cost of goods sold is more than thirty percent, that can also get a little scary. Think about your admin cost and your office and work to understand the acceptable expense ratios. That way, as you grow, if those expense ratios hold true throughout the growth, then you're fine. Ideally, at some point, you get economies of scale, and that's when margin gets created. So managing cash flow, I'd say, is the first big mistake that I made.

My second big mistake is not hiring the right people fast enough.

Dan: Let's talk more about that. What does that mean? What does that look like? You're growing, you feel like you're hitting your head against the ceiling, but you're not willing to take the risk to hire somebody. How did that show up for you?

Ryan: It appeared in two ways. Number one, when you really need to hire the people, you rarely can afford to do it. So you're looking and you're saying, "We're doing everything we can right now. The team is hustling. Everybody is working, and we're right there on the brink. We need to breakthrough, and we just can't afford to hire this person."

In my experience, that's rarely the case. When we look at people, let's say it's a high-dollar, executive-level person, they're going to cost you £100,000 a year. Safe to say that's a well-paid person.

What you must keep in mind is that you don't pay that person £100,000 the first day they walk into the building. People come with a 12-month finance plan. If they don't pay off, if they don't offer ROI – and the expensive ones should do so relatively quickly — then you let them go. You encourage them to pursue opportunities elsewhere.

The key is to think about people not in terms of what they cost over the year, but their cost between the day you hire them and the day you expect them to produce a positive ROI for the business.

The more expensive they're going to be, then, frankly, the faster they should ROI because they have experience and high-value skills. They should walk in very, very quickly and have an immediate impact.

Remember, rarely is it easy to hire. You think, "I can't afford that person," but if you look at it, you can. There are ways to manage it. Maybe you need to re-allocate resources. Maybe you need to let good people go to hire great people. That's really hard to do, but it's critical. The feeling that I can't afford to hire people to take me to the next level is one I think gazelles feel all the time. It's perfectly normal. But it's one you must get past if you want to grow. The way I get past it is to look very closely at expenses and finding the money? And then comes the acknowledgement that it's okay if it feels uncomfortable because you're a fast-growth company.

The second thing to keep in mind when it comes to people is they're never going to be as good as you, which is really hard. It's easier when you're hiring for a position you know nothing about. At every company I've been with, I've had to hire people to do the thing that I felt was my core competency, and so, as a business owner, you must identify your core competency, the thing you do very, very well.

For me, it's on the marketing side. I'm a marketer first. I like writing sales copy. I love producing offers. I like getting my hands dirty and setting up ad campaigns, writing follow up series. I'm good at it. It's a pretty high-leverage activity, but I can't continue to do that if I want the company to scale. I have to bring people in to do that. And so to have that realisation that they're never going to be as good as you is something you just have to accept and be okay with.

But at the same time, I'm not telling you to settle. It's not about settling for people that aren't as good as you. It's about acknowledging that you're actually good at probably half a dozen things.

On the marketing side, there's the media-buying traffic side, there's the copywriting side, there's the product side, and there's the offer creation side. And while I don't believe that there's anyone in my office today that is as good as me at all of those things, I believe there are individuals that are better at those component parts than I am because they get to focus on just that. And so you have to get over that.

If you're the founder of Excel, then you're good. You should be proud of that. But finding specialists and tacticians that are good at that particular thing is very doable. So to start building your team based on those pieces, then what you wind up with is what I have today. When I look at my office, I see a group of people far better in aggregate at doing the things I think I'm pretty great at. When that situation is in place for you, that's when you have the ability to scale.

Dan: *As you've gone from seven figures, to eight to nine, how have your problems changed? How have they evolved?*

Ryan: Funny enough, they haven't. The problem is always running up against the same two things that I mentioned before – cash flow. You always reach a no-man's land, a point where you're too small to be big, and too big to be small. So you reach that point and you have to really make a commitment – a commitment to people and a commitment to margin. A commitment to power through.

When you're trudging through the desert, you're not throwing parties. You're not popping champagne bottles. You're moving, one foot in front of the other, walking until you get through it. The goal is to get to the other side. And the way you get to the other side is learning to manage cash flow. It's about identifying the people you need, figuring out how to on-board them and integrate them into the current staff. And then, it's about creating systems that will take you to the next level.

So at each level, in addition to cash flow and people, you also have systems issues. Systems can be in the form of technology. We used to use shared servers, but we can't use them anymore. We'll crash them. So then we got our own server, but even that wasn't good enough. We had to have a series of servers, each one pinging the other. That's a significantly different expense each time. The same is true for our shopping cart solutions. My very first email marketing solution used to just broadcast my list was about $18/month. Today, we spend over $75,000 every single month just to broadcast emails to our different lists.

It is a fundamentally different level each time, but you have to manage cash flow. What matters is gathering the people who will be with you on that trudge through the desert and establishing the systems that will take you there. You have to really codify your processes. When you're going to the next level, if you don't have a good plan and a good process in place, you're going to die out in the desert, and then you have to manage cash flow until you get to the other side, reach that inflection point where you get those economies of scale, and start spinning off cash again.

In that time, you also have to remain humble because you know it's coming again soon. If you continue to grow, it's coming again soon.

Dan: *Right, and that makes sense, doesn't it? You've got to hire the people first. It's cause and effect; you've got to get the people, you've got to get things in place to get to the next level. But when you reach that level, you haven't got what you need to get to the level beyond that.*

Ryan: When we first hit a million dollars, it was great. From about a million to about three to five million, it was pretty good. And then the five to 10 million was terrible. We hit 10 million and life was pretty good, 10 to 12 million was okay, and then, until we got to 25 million, it was terrible.

This last year, we went through another no man's land. Now that we're on the other side of 50 million, things are pretty good. We'll see how long that lasts because we're moving really quickly to a hundred million, so I get to find out where that next no man's land lies and when it will get really, really hard again. But that's just part of it.

But I know I'm going to encounter those same things. At every level, it's going to be the same things, the same types of problems. I've dealt with it before, just at a different scale. It's just another zero.

Dan: *Do you have any final words of wisdom you would give to any aspiring gazelles?*

Ryan: Yeah, two things. Number one, concerns managing a team as you grow. Most gazelles have the hardest time dealing with this because finding great people takes a long time and on-boarding and training great people appropriately takes a long time. If there's one thing gazelles don't have, it's time.

So, when it comes to bringing on great people, we practice the 10-80-10 philosophy. It can be very difficult to let go completely, and when you do bring somebody on, especially if they're going to take over a true core competency of yours, then don't just abdicate control. Number one, it's hard to do, and number two, it's dangerous. Your abilities are part of the magic that led to that growth. So don't completely abdicate control.

I recommend, in the beginning, that you work with the new person on 10 percent. So if we're talking about rolling out a new product line, you be there and come up with the general idea – the name, the concept, all the stuff. Tell them what you want it to do. Come up with a theme. If it's a new offer, maybe you're creating the headline, the lead. Whatever you're really great at, be there for that first critical 10 percent to set the stage, set the vision, and create the parameters, then let them go. Have them do 80 percent, which is where the bulk of the work is, and then you come back and do the last 10 percent to plus it and approve it.

And when you do that enough times, there will eventually come a time that, instead of you doing the first 10, you ask the person, "So what do you think?" And what they throw out to you is exactly what you would do, sometimes better. Great, now you can ignore that first 10 percent and go to a 90-10. Tell them, "You just do it and let me know what you're thinking and check in." Eventually, you'll be saying, "Let me know when you want me to take a look at it." And then there's going to come a day when they bring you something you didn't know they were going to bring you and you've got no way to plus it at all. After they do that a couple of times, you say, "You know what, you got this. Call me if you want to."

And that's how we've been able to scale talents of people through all the different roles using the 10-80-10, then 90-10, then eventually the 100 percent system.

The other thing I would tell gazelles to remember is that the secret to scaling is to avoid surprises, which means getting good at guessing. You need to have projections about where you believe you'll be in twelve months, including a month to month plan detailing how you'll get there. Lay out the amount of revenue you believe you'll make and what you believe the expenses to be.

The first time you do it, it's going to feel like the stupidest thing in the world because you won't have anything to base it on. It's just guessing, and that's fine. Guess. Make assumptions. And then when you're wrong, you get to learn why you were wrong. You'll learn from that, and you'll get better next time, and the next year, you'll be able to do it a little better. Eventually, you'll know what should happen, so that if any little thing goes wrong, you'll sense it and see a problem coming in the future. Limiting surprises is the key to scale. Surprises kill.

CHAPTER 2

SET FOR LIFE?

"Good enough never is."

—— DEBBI FIELDS

"Dan, Dan, are you okay?"

It's my wife.

"You've been in an accident."

I'm in the hospital. The last thing I remember is racing down a hill on my bike.

In 2011, as a hobby, I took up triathlons with one of my employees, Kevin. We'd started off with sprint triathlons and then upgraded to Olympic distance. Then I said, "I want to lose some weight. Let's do a half Ironman."

70.3 miles. That is the total distance of a half Ironman triathlon.

1.2 mile swim,

56 mile bike ride,

13.1 mile half-marathon run.

It is the hardest thing I've ever done physically. Kevin and I finished, but my brother-in-law Lee failed to make the cut-off time, so I said to him, "I'll do it again with you next year."

That second year, I am underprepared and undertrained, especially on the bike. The bike is my least favourite; it requires the longest amount of training time and hurts the most. The muscles, the saddle sores. You can't sit down, your crotch gets bruised; it's not fun.

I push myself to try and meet the cut-off. If I don't reach the transition from swim to bike and bike to run by the cut-off time, then I can't continue the race. I watch the clock; I can do math fast. I figure out exactly the pace needed to make it in time, and I realise I can only just make it by the skin of my teeth. I am pushing, and it is the hardest thing I've ever done in my life. On a pain scale of one to ten, ten being agonising, I am at an eight for most of the four-hour bike ride.

As I cruise down a hill, legs burning with lactic acid, heart racing, and lungs heavy, I can't catch my breath. My lack of training means I am inhaling large amounts of air and exhaling loudly. And I'm worried about that cut-off time. I'm in a wooded area, surrounded by trees, and the sun is shining. I am flying down this bumpy, country lane, and the next thing I remember, I am opening my eyes in the hospital and my wife is calling my name.

The next few months are very blurry for me.

I find out later that my tire burst and flung me head first into a tree. I hit the tree so hard that my helmet split in half. I ended up, literally, with brain damage, what is known as a traumatic brain injury, TBI.

It is, without a doubt, the worst period of my life. I am in and out of comas for weeks, and in and out of hospital for a few months. Even when I get out of the hospital, my brain is foggy, and I feel as if I am on a bad anaesthesia for months. I have always been very emotionally stable, but in this period,

I get insanely paranoid. I don't sleep, and I have the attention span of a goldfish. Basic, everyday tasks, like figuring out how to use a computer, become very difficult. It is a challenging time in my life.

In her TED Talk *My Stroke of Insight*, Jill Bolte Taylor, a brain scientist, describes herself having a stroke. She watches as her brain functions—motion, speech, self-awareness—shut down one by one. It was like that for me, literally. I could feel my mental faculty slipping away, and this was weeks after the actual event.

At one point, I go severely downhill and think I am going to die. There is bleeding, I have surgery, and I can remember one night where I am heavily medicated and nothing seems real, like my own personal version of the film *Inception*. It feels like I am living in dream layers; I am seeing visions of bad things happening…a premonition of the house burning down or a plane overhead creating the belief that an alien spaceship is landing. It doesn't feel like I am all there. This night, it is scary, unsettling, and precarious.

The accident caused a profound shift in me for many reasons. I had been a successful business owner and high-income earner for nine years prior to my accident, and at the time, I had two children. I realised that night that if I died or ended up like a vegetable, my family would not be set for life. Yes, there were some savings, and yes, there was insurance, but give it a few years, and my wife would have had to go back to work.

I will never forget that night, the moment I realised that my family should be set for life but they weren't. For hours, I lay there, questioning what the hell I had been doing for the previous nine years.

Obviously, I didn't die. I still have my faculty (although that still can be debated by some people in my life). After my recovery, I realised I had to sort this out. I had income, but I had not been creating wealth. My level of personal wealth relative to what I should have had, given my years of sustained high income, was pathetic.

Good Enough Will Not Get You There

I decided to turn things around and became obsessive about building assets and building businesses. I had two businesses at the time, and both survived. The blessing was that I had created enough systems in the companies, and they were successful *enough* to run without me, so I didn't go broke. It took me seven or eight months to recover fully before I was able to get back to work properly and pick them up again.

My businesses were solid enough, so I had done a good job at scaling them. Every business owner needs to build a solid business that can exist without him. But my business was severely and negatively impacted because I had not done a *good enough job*. They both took a hit, and weren't far away from going under. If I had been out any longer — a year or two — it would have been game over for both of my businesses. I had been running my business just like I had been training for that second Ironman, underprepared and undertrained. It was enough to get by, but I was at risk.

As I was convalescing and recovering, gradually getting my mental faculty back, I couldn't concentrate for long periods of time and consequently had a lot of time to sit and do some critical thinking. I thought about what was happening within the business and how could I fix it. *What do I need to do to build a business that works, that is not dependent upon me, that's stronger, more profitable, that doesn't have underachieving employees, or this stinking, ongoing cash crisis?*

In my first month back at work, the business made more profit than it had made in the previous year. The profit increase was so dramatic because I spent the better part of seven months thinking about what I needed to do to really fix the business.

What about you? Are you running your business like I trained for my Ironman? Do you have structures or training schedules in place? Maybe you have targets and goals set, but you aren't following them. Are you pushing it? Maybe you can make it to the next quarter, the next milestone, the next cut off, but will it nearly kill you? Will it split your helmet in half?

Are you working in inefficient, ineffective ways that keep you from properly providing for, and enjoying, your family? Are you wasting time? Are you ready to build real wealth and quality of life?

The way I chose to build wealth was to exit one of the companies. If you build your business to sell, you will maximise the value of the business, allowing you to sell it for the largest amount of money. It is given the highest valuation when it is maximally profitable and stable. The risks have been mitigated, and the business is less dependent on you, making it a reliable, predictable, sustainable profit. Then, if you keep the business, your life is easier, you have more money, and you have more time. If you exit, you're exiting for the largest amount of money.

Even if you have no intention of selling and exiting your business, you should build it with the intent to exit because your opinion might change, or you might have a health challenge. And if you run your business from an investor perspective, you're going to make more money yourself. You can still choose to work in your business, especially if you love being hands-on the way I do, but do it because you want to, not because you have to.

With one of my businesses, one year and 17 days after my accident, I sold the company. The accident was on June 17, 2012. On June 30, 2013, two weeks before my 30th birthday, I exited the company for £1.05 million.

Now there is enough money in investments to take care of my children.

Keep reading, and I will teach you these strategies.

Interview with Sean Greeley

Now, we'll hear from Sean Greeley, CEO of NPE, which was founded in July of 1996. The company has gone from two employees in 1996 to three offices around the world – Orlando, London, and Sydney — and a staff of about 65 total globally. NPE has served over 21,000 customers in 94 countries, helping them grow their business to the next level. His company has been listed six years running in the *Inc. 500/5000* list, and were the UK National Business awards finalist in 2015. Interestingly, in addition to understanding the path to becoming a gazelle, Sean's business path, like mine, was strongly influenced by a serious health issue.

Dan: *Sean, tell me how you became a gazelle. Your company has had such rapid growth. Where did this fast growth start?*

Sean: In terms of my story, I was an athlete and then a coach, and I owned a fitness company. I grew it for myself to two locations and a staff of eight coaches in central Florida. I was rated one of the top five personal trainers in America in 2005. I really enjoyed growing a fitness company, but I was trying to figure out what was next for me. Did I want to go do a third location, a fourth location? Did I want to franchise? For me, if I'm not facing big challenges, I'm kind of bored and looking for more. I was definitely at that point with my fitness company.

I had a really unexpected life change when a freckle on my forehead turned dark, and I got a check-up. The doctor said I had stage IV melanoma cancer. It absolutely changed my life. I sold my businesses and took some time to focus on my health. At that point, I didn't know if I was going to live or even be around in a year or two. After several months working with my oncologist, I had surgery, and they took out a bunch of lymph nodes. One lab said the results were bad, one lab said they were good, and third lab said they were inconclusive, all of which really told me nothing. I worked with my doctor and looked after my health, and now I'm fortunate to be 12 years cancer-free.

Not knowing if I was going to live or not at a young age changed the course of my life. After selling my business and focusing on my health, I decided I just wanted to help people, especially if I might not be around that long. I had no other vision other than wanting to help people.

I had a lot of friends who were coaches and fitness business owners, who had small gyms and fitness centres and struggling with different aspects of their business—marketing, sales, staff, and managing finances. On instinct, I just started helping them. It really wasn't a business model. Rather, it was me helping some people, doing some consulting, and putting on a couple of workshops. That led me to Dan Kennedy and the GKIC community, and I bought a couple of books and got the newsletter. I got an invitation to come to the Info-Summit in November

'06, and I really saw a vision of how to take knowledge work or consulting and put a business model around that.

I learned about membership sites, licensing programs, franchising, information products, subscription newsletters, and coaching/consulting, all of which helped me to see ways to structure and put a business model around what I thought was helping people and sharing my knowledge. I also learned a lot about direct response marketing and about technology and sales and marketing automation. I really enjoyed the experience, since I'm naturally passionate about learning and growth and the application of knowledge.

My new understanding led to launching a subscription program. Within three weeks of that seminar, I put a hundred people into $100 a month subscription for a business advice mentorship program. Then things took off. The company grew very organically as we focused on getting really in tune with the problems our clients and customers were struggling with, and then giving them solutions. Oftentimes, we were able to create the solution and package it in a way that we could train it, deliver it, and grow them to the next level.

NPE took off. It went from $60,000 revenue in year one ('06) with barely a profit because the vision wasn't developed and I had to deal with the expenses of a new business, to $850,000 the next year. I think year three was $2.1 million, followed by $3.4 million the next year, and it just kept going. We've just finished up 2015 with a little over $10 million in revenue for the year. I'm pleased about that. It's been quite a run.

Dan: *I'm curious, Sean. I know that you are very committed and passionate about learning, about constantly growing and improving, so what have been your biggest lessons along the way, or what have been some of your biggest failures or mistakes?*

Sean: Great question. Biggest lessons, I'd say, have been about entrepreneurship and the major, major challenges we faced at multiple points in the business's lifespan and growth. These challenges are really hard in growing a company, since they make you question why you're doing what you're doing and whether it's really worth it. It's quite hard to go back to a smaller company and keep it really simple.

You've got to make a decision: are you going back down or are you going to double down and go all in?

At every point, I've doubled down and gone back in. I've really recommitted myself and my team and grown as a leader, as well as a man. It's important to be willing to be humble and to ask for help, and it's amazing how, when you're willing to do that, there are incredible mentors out there, entrepreneurs who have handled every challenge you face and felt the same pressure and struggle you are feeling. They want to help because they've been there, they've lived through it, and they know the pain.

We tell people to have courage and practice faith through that process and through that journey. It's amazing to realise that every problem has a solution. It's completely normal at every stage of growth to be dealing with whatever challenges you're dealing with. It's incredible to go through those experiences, to face big challenges, and to overcome them. I don't think there's any better feeling than enjoying that success with people you enjoy working with and you care about, all the while knowing you're making a difference in the world.

Dan: *I know you've had a lot of mentors, Sean. How did you seek out those mentors? How did you choose the right mentor? What's the best piece of advice a mentor has ever given you?*

Sean: I've been a really committed student. I've invested hundreds of thousands of dollars in my education, self-education through workshops, seminars, consultants. You should see my library. Any book, course, or DVD, I've got it. I have really enjoyed that process.

As far as mentors, there have been different key people at different stages of the business's growth and different stages of my growth. Dan Kennedy has been a great mentor to me. I've spent a lot of time with him as a private client for some time as well.

As I'm growing a bigger company, the size we are today with the challenges we face, certainly Clate Mask is one of my greatest mentors and someone I look up to. The whole executive team at Infusionsoft has been awesome to me. They have been great friends in my life and really supported me personally, and our organisation, in working through some of the phases of growth, particularly as we crossed that chasm of five to ten million and prepared to go over the $10 million mark. They've been there, done that, so they've lived those experiences and know about the journey. They have generously shared their experiences and helped me to navigate that.

Dan: *In talking about the journey, Sean, we know that there are different stages that businesses go through as they grow and expand. Have your problems changed, and, if so, how have they changed as you've grown?*

Sean: Constantly. Do we have eight hours? It's a long story to articulate all those pieces. I think some of the most memorable are times when the marketing really stopped working, and stopped working in terms of evolving the brand and repositioning some of our company and products. Though we'd been able to grow to a certain point at that level, it then needed to be re-sharpened to continue to go to the next level.

It was also important to replace myself in certain areas of the business, finding a director of marketing, for example. I can't tell you how many years that took to get in place, to find someone I felt comfortable having take over that leadership. The same thing is true in sales and in services. Really, it's true at every function of the business: finding the key hire, finding the key leader of that team, and then growing the team.

I remember when I had to write all the copy. And I remember the first time I got a copywriter. I actually started with a full-time copywriter, then went to a bunch of freelancers, then had no one, and then hired another full-time writer. It was so important to find someone that I really trusted to represent the voice, and really my voice, as well as having the right creative team, especially because I'm passionate about marketing. I'm good at it; I understand it well. So having people you trust who can represent you and replace you in those functions is huge.

There's not been anything that's been easy. It's all hard. It's all challenging all the time. I think it gets more and more fun as you add great people to your organisation, real leaders who can take a ball and run with it and that you can trust and grow with over time. That's been awesome, and it continues to make it more fun because you can let go of certain functions of the business and start to play a more strategic role. That continues to grow over time, and I'm enjoying the progression. I wouldn't be here if I hadn't also worked through and enjoyed, even though they were hard, all the other stages along the way.

It's crucial to be grateful in the process, even when dealing with a tough phase or a tough challenge, and to be able to enjoy that, because of the times that make you who you are and that you remember along the way. When you look back, you can see how you got to where you are today.

Dan: As you're transitioning through the ten million mark now, Sean, what are you still working on in your business? What challenges are you pushing up against and breaking through at the moment?

Sean: A few things, some strategic pieces. We have a global business, which means the business never sleeps. There is always an office open. There are always people working. Things are always happening in Orlando, in London, in Sydney. I didn't go looking for those opportunities. They really found me.

I can remember, probably in 2007, getting a fax—back when we actually got faxes—and they were from some guys in Australia who wanted to license the business there. We had a series of meetings and negotiations, did our due diligence, and ended up licensing our products to be sold in Australia. These guys grew it to a certain place, and then got stuck and the growth levelled off. I made a deal about two and a half years ago to take that back over and then restructured some parts of that business. I moved it from Perth to Sydney, and I started to scale the company and the team there.

In London, I had people calling me, wanting us to come to the UK. I pushed it off for a long time, then eventually decided to do a test. After the test, things started to take off and I put an office there.

But learning how all the parts of your business report in and fit together, how the teams work together, and how to manage a global business was a big learning curve for me and for my team. I didn't have it all figured out from the start, that's for sure.

We recently changed our sales strategy to give us two sales channels, a phone channel and a live events channel. We've also scaled our presenter team to create a global team and based our phone team in Orlando and changed to a shift model. Now we have a morning and evening shift with staff on the sales floor for about 18 to 20 hours a day. That allows us to sell to the world out of one office, reduce our management costs, and really get the team and culture aligned to feed that energy. That's been a beneficial transition.

Certainly, we're seeing a lot of acceleration as a result, as opposed to some of our earlier methods. Global management is not easy. Some team members and departments work well virtually, while other team members really work well when they're all in an office together and feed off one another. Sales is one of those departments. We just made that transition and we're already seeing great benefit and return in just the last few months. I'm excited for that to continue.

Dan: For the reader reading this who is not yet a gazelle — perhaps they are slightly less than a million in revenue but looking to break through to that seven-figure level and continue with the fast growth — what advice would you give them?

Sean: A few things. Number one, stay humble. For a lot of people, ego gets in the way at a certain point and they think they know it all because they're the most successful they have ever been. They're making more money than they have in their entire lives. They think they're amazing. But that's when you're ready for a fall. You don't know it all. There's always something around the corner waiting to smack you down. Stay humble.

Stay hungry. Spend time learning and growing your leadership skills. We have a saying: if you're the smartest person in the room, you're in the wrong room. Make sure you spend time with people who are ahead of where you are, who inspire you, and who can support you in your journey.

It's very easy to get sucked into the growth of the business and hitting numbers and forget the core of what you do and how you create amazing value for your customers. Whether through services, products, or software, continually focus on not just growth, but on quality growth, quality customer acquisition, and on customer retention.

At the core, if you love your customers and love your team, and you put as much as you can into that effort, then it's unbelievable how everything else just works. You'll figure out the business challenges along the way. If you take that approach, you can't help but stand out in the marketplace because people know you're amazing. They appreciate you. They value you. They tell other people about you. They stick around, and they never want to leave.

Learn how to love your customers more and more every day. Don't let your ego get in the way of making tough decisions. Be willing to be humble and accept criticism and improvement where you can. The same is true with your team. Find really great people you can attract to your organisation, people with whom you love working and that you trust. Then go have fun together and do great things. I think that's what it's all about. When you're having fun, your team's having fun, and you're loving customers, it just gets better and better at every turn.

Dan: *Is there anything we've not discussed that you'd like to share with gazelles or aspiring gazelles?*

Sean: Be patient. I'm very passionate about growth, but I've learned in the last ten years to have more patience today than ever. When you're growing a business, reaching the level of gazelle and beyond, it's a marathon, not a sprint. The journey takes a lot of mental toughness and patience and persistence. It's all about the mental game you play with yourself, about expectations and how you meet them, and how you recover from setbacks and challenges along the way. Work hard to be patient and remember to have fun.

I think it's all too easy to get caught up in the game and forget to have fun, which then leaves you frustrated when you don't hit every mark at every point. Honestly, you learn more from the things you don't accomplish on time than the things you do because it allows you to look within, to look around, and to find ways to improve. So again, be patient and have as much fun as you can along the way. You only go around once. Enjoy the ride.

CHAPTER 3

CRITICAL ELEMENTS TO SUCCESS

"There are three constants in life...
change, choice and principles."

—— STEPHEN COVEY

To get to the next level, to get from half a million to £10 million plus in revenue, there are three critical elements.

The first is key principles, a new level of thinking to get you from where you are today to where you want to be. There are some core tenants that you must understand and operate in to perform at this higher level.

The second part is strategy. These principles show you how to analyse a business and how to look at it differently. Doing so allows you to design the optimal strategy for the maximum possible return on investment, to be able to scale up.

Finally, you have to execute. Execution is critical. Most people never have a coherent plan because they have not done it with the right principles. And even if you have a coherent, strategic plan, the results depend upon how effectively the plan is executed. In this section, you'll find a few simple things you can do immediately to allow your level of productivity and output radically improve and help you execute better than you have ever done before.

In the principles section, we'll discuss three key things. The first is the power of critical thinking. Business is an intellectual sport and most people don't know how to analyse their business. They spend their time and energy solving the wrong problem, which will never yield the desired outcome. If you run east looking for a sunset, you're going to have a problem.

Secondly, we're going to talk about the power of mastermind. This is the ultimate leverage. If you want to solve any problem, remember that there are so many people out there to consult, people who can help you do it quicker and more easily, while sparing you the pain of figuring it out yourself.

Finally, there's the multiplier effect. Your business chain is only as strong as its weakest link. If you understand what levers to pull, making tiny micro adjustments in each of these key areas of your business, you'll find these are pivot points, leverage points. If altered, a slight adjustment in each of these areas will have radical, compounded, geometric impact on your bottom line profitability. That's the principles section.

Once you've done the analysis, the deep thinking on your business, you can move into section two, which is about the strategy, the strategic plan.

Here, we're going to talk about four things. We'll discuss financial analysis, how to analyse the scoreboard of your business. We'll tackle business value maximisation, a simple tool to locate the low hanging fruit in your business so you can immediately capitalise on it.

We'll talk about maximising your return on investment by analysing your business' performance and processes easily to leverage your business through people and systems.

Lastly, the above information will allow you to create a comprehensive, strategic plan for the next quarter in which you best allocate your resources to get the maximum possible return on investment.

Once you've done that and you have the right strategy, you'll be into part three, which is execution. There are three critical elements to the proper execution of your plan. The first is recruitment, training, and getting the maximum performance out of your people. Next is the creation of the right metrics in your business, the leading indicators that will allow you to hold people accountable to maximum performance.

Finally, we'll deal with your personal productivity. In this chapter, we'll talk about the simplest, easiest way to get this implemented into your business, resulting in more cash in your bank account at the end of this month.

Your Biggest Obstacles To Success

There are only two things that stand in your way. The first is time. The reason you are in this mess is because you're spending your time on the wrong things, solving the wrong problems. Everybody has the same amount of time, so it's not about lack; it's that you are spending time doing the wrong things. Ultimately, you are allocating and therefore wasting that time on ineffective strategies. Overcoming this obstacle means eliminating the unnecessary distractions that take 80 percent of your time and have no positive impact on your bottom line.

I will help you identify effective strategies so you can immediately, radically, cut wasted time and either save time off or reallocate that time into the strategies offering the highest possible return. Not having the time is bull. The amount of hours in the day represents one of the few constants amongst all people, and I'm going to show you how to best use those hours.

The second obstacle is money. Again, the reason you find yourself in this situation is because you are not executing things in the right way. However, if you're going to try to tell me that, once your business is bigger, once it's more successful, *then* you will implement this stuff, you might as well stop reading right now. The fact is, money is not an effect, it's an output.

To say you will get the money and *then* you will hire the people you need is putting the cart before the horse. It's just not possible to do that. But, if you allocate your time correctly into the right strategies, you are putting the causes in place that will allow your business to gain momentum, to turn around, and ease the cash flow. It will increase the profit margins or bring in more customers, which will then create the effect, or the money, you're after.

Creating Time Where There Is None

Joe had a low seven-figure business, running a digital marketing agency in the West Midlands. He specialised in running social media marketing campaigns and building ecommerce platforms for clients.

It was doing, at one point, £2 million in revenue. Joe was tired and burnt out. He was working 70-80 hour weeks. He had been growing so fast that there was no profit. There was never any money at the end of the month. It was a constant battle.

The necessary changes were very apparent to me, but he was so busy trying to fulfil on client projects that he didn't feel he could take the time to execute upon the strategies I was giving him. On top of that, he felt like he didn't have the money to make the shifts. When he had some money, he told me, *then* he could afford to hire the people to lessen his workload, to make it all fit.

More specifically, he came in thinking that, if only he could get more clients, then it would all magically work. Once I did a proper analysis and identified the problem, the reality emerged, which was that he tried to scale up the business by hiring additional staff, believing he would make more profit by outsourcing to contractors, but when the number of clientele dipped slightly, he still had to pay the staff, so he radically ate through his profit. The real issue was the clients weren't paying him the right level of fee, and they caused a lot of hassle and aggravation, so the profit margin wasn't there.

Honestly, by just creating a little bit of time, a few quiet hours to converse and do the critical thinking, we were able to immediately see a very significant leverage point. This leverage point allowed him to save almost ten hours per week by cutting out clients who were taking up a lot of his time but not actually making any profit. In addition, he was able to identify further savings that increased the profit by almost £30,000 a month.

He went from a break-even business, with a huge amount of stress, to less hours and radically more money. All because he applied the principles I will cover in this book to allow him to better analyse the real problem. He implemented the right strategies and executed upon them, and as a result, got radically more money for less time invested.

The real issue wasn't about having enough clients coming consistently enough, and it wasn't about being able to hire better people more cheaply. The real issue was about being able to find the right quality clients. Immediately, the process turned transformative when he eliminated a significant number of clients who were just wasting time.

The real issue wasn't about having enough clients coming consistently enough, and it wasn't about being able to hire better people more cheaply. The real issue was about being able to find the right quality clients.

When we analysed the actual hours spent for the money made, Joe's company was losing money. He was working 80 hours and making £X, when he could have been making 2X working 60 hours, but unfortunately, that second earning scenario was out of reach. As Joe's situation illustrates, if you have a problem in your business and you attempt to grow the business, you're just exasperating the problem. That's was his exact strategy before he applied the principles that allowed him to identify the root cause and the real issue in his business.

Once the problem was identified, getting the right strategy in place, and then executing it, was comparatively easy. Same business, radically different results.

PART I

PRINCIPLES

OVERVIEW OF THE FOUR PRINCIPLES

The following four principles are the cornerstones of all business success. The first is critical thinking. My mentor, Keith J. Cunningham, taught me that business is an intellectual sport, and most business owners are going with gut instinct, which then leaves them feeling surprised when they get killed.

Business is an intellectual chess game, and you have to move multiple pieces around simultaneously. You need to be able to identify the real problem, the root cause, rather than dealing with symptoms. Just as I outlined in the previous example with my client, Joe, it is crucial to address the real, critical problems in your business to get the results that you want. *Your business is only as strong as its weakest link.* You have to identify that weak link so as not to waste energy and to maximise your return on investment.

The second cornerstone principle is the power of mastermind. There is a famous quote in business, "If you're the smartest person in the room, you're in the wrong room." Your job should be to become the dumbest person in the room, learning from people who have already accomplished what you want to accomplish. Not only does that help you get better results without making the mistakes yourself, you speed to solution. This is the game changer in today's business climate, when the marketplace is moving so quickly you can't figure it out yourself. You have to leverage other people. Speed to solution by learning lessons, good and bad, from other players in your industry. Doing so raises the bar on your own play as well.

The third principle is deal flow. The person who has the best options has the best life, and having good comparisons is the key. If you're trying to buy a house, how do you know if it's worth the valuation put on it? You look at other comparable houses. If you've looked at a hundred other houses in that area with the same square footage and the same number of bedrooms, you'll have a hundred references as to whether the price they're quoting is a good price or a bad price, if it's a good deal or a bad deal.

You need to get deal flow in order to make the best choice. Having the discipline to get deal flow on your business decisions is the difference between having a good business and a failing business, just as it's the difference between having a good business and a great business. Rather than getting okay employees, get extraordinary employees. The secret is deal flow.

The fourth and final principle is the multiplier effect. I don't believe in 'get rich quick', and you shouldn't either. However, you can get geometric results. The key is to identify the leverage points in your business, the little adjustments that make a huge impact on the next stage in the process. Identify those leverage points, measure them, and then kick the can, meaning that you must incrementally increase those leverage points.

For example, sales is an output (or an effect) caused by five different inputs or leverage points. Those leverage points are:

Crowd—how many people know your business exists,

Capture Rate—how many people actively engage and show an interest in your product or service,

Conversion Rate—what percentage of the people make a purchase,

Cash Value—how much money they spend on average, and

Continuity Rate—how frequently they come back to repurchase. If you incrementally increase these five inputs, you'll get a geometric increase in the output.

If you're able to double each of the five inputs (e.g., increase the Capture Rate from 8 percent to 16 percent, increase the Conversion Rate from 1.2 percent to 2.4 percent, etc.), you'll get a 32x effect on your sales revenue.

In other words, if your business is currently doing £100,000, these five changes will increase your revenue to £3.2 million! This is exactly what I did with one of my early businesses. Those are numbers worth some thought, wouldn't you say?

So, how do you identify those leverage points that will create the multiplier effect in your business? The steps are discussed, in detail, later in this book.

So there you have it, the cornerstones of business success. As a successful business owner, the four key principles that you most live by are critical thinking, the power of mastermind, getting deal flow, and the multiplier effect.

THE FIVE Cs

		BEFORE	AFTER
👥 **CROWD**	X	10,000	20,000
💰 **CAPTURE**	%	10	20
🔄 **CONVERSION**	%	10	20
🪙 **CASH VALUE**	£	1,000	2,000
⚙ **CONTINUITY**	X	1	2

	BEFORE	AFTER
= SALES	£100,000	**£3,200,000**

Interview with Steve Bolton

Steve Bolton is the founder and executive chairman of Platinum Partners Group of companies which includes Platinum Property Partners, the fastest growing premium franchise in UK history. That business currently has 250 franchise partners, owns more than £200 million worth of property, and more than 4,000 housemates are living in a PPP property today.

Additional businesses include Platinum E-Commerce Partners, a new but successful and proven franchise opportunity helping people make money in e-commerce, specifically starting with Amazon; Platinum Rooms, a series of residential property funds for passive investment; and Platinum Asset Management, which handles serviced offices, business centres, hotels, residential and commercial development projects.

Steve also has a charity, Peace One Day, which was recently thrust into the limelight for taking the government to court by a judicial review to overturn what it considered an unintelligent, unfair and unlawful tax legislation.

Dan: *Steve, tell me the story of how your first business had rapid growth and then fell on its face. I think there's a lot to be learned from starting at the beginning.*

Steve: When I first started doing over a million in revenue, I had two businesses back in the '90s. One was a management training business and one was an adventure construction company. We were experiencing far more than twenty percent annualised growth, which kicked off in about 1997. It was the right product, the right time, and a good team of people.

Of course, it all came crashing down in 2001 because of September 11th and the foot and mouth disease caused by the terror attacks in New York. Foot and mouth disease stopped our construction teams from being able to build the climbing walls and ropes courses that were essential to our business. So that company had to be put into voluntary liquidation.

And then the management training and consulting business, which involved outdoors team-building activities for big, blue chip companies, was also affected by the events of September 11th. We were heavily exposed to the financial services sector and did a lot of graduate training and management training for the banking sector. Because of 9/11, many of those organisations had their entertainment and training budgets cut. My business went from making close to half a million pound a year net profit back to breaking even. We had to shed a load of staff.

I call that the best worst experience of my life. It was very painful. I had to sell my five-bedroom family home and move into rented accommodation with my wife, who was seven months pregnant. Yes, I had a gazelle company nearly 20 years ago, two of them really. But because of factors outside of our control, we basically had to start all over again.

Dan: *What were the biggest lessons that you took away from that, Steve?*

Steve: The biggest lessons included understanding that you've got to be really mindful of risk in business, and that there are very real risks; some are predictable, some are completely unpredictable. It just taught me about resilience. There is the old saying in America that the average millionaire loses everything three times before he eventually learns how to keep hold of it. That was me. I was a millionaire on paper, then lost it all, virtually overnight, within about a three-month time frame.

I went from being a naturally optimistic, go-getting, gung ho, risk-taking entrepreneur to being cautious and sceptical, which is a much better balance, I would say. I think one of the lessons is recognising that I've had business partners before who were very operational, very corporate. They look at risk all the time, always predicting what was going to go wrong, and they're incredibly valuable people to have as part of a team. But typically, those people never start a business. They never take the risk.

If there's a pendulum between very high risk and very low risk, I ended up somewhere around the middle. I became a lot more sensitive to the industries and sectors I dealt with. I learned to not be reliant on just one customer. My recommendation is to look at what's going on:

- Internally with systems and processes
- In your industry
- In the big, wide world - study the macro picture in the wider world.

What may or may not impact you and your business?

The key change for me was that I became a lot more cautious. I started to analyse risks a lot more, and I sought out business models that were much more robust and resilient, which is why I ended up in two fields. One was property and the other was franchising, simply because they are two of the most tried, tested, and proven. They have the lowest levels of volatility out of the majority of businesses that I could find.

Dan: *What is the single best piece of advice you ever received from a mentor?*

Steve: It depends on where I was in my mentor journey. I think mentors are incredibly valuable, but sometimes the mentor role can also be filled by a book, or one line of advice from someone you meet. When I was starting out, I had a full-time job. While everyone told me not to give up the security of that job, at the time, I was fed up with it. A friend of my dad's essentially told me to go for it and said, "Look, what's the worst that can happen? You can always go back to having a job. You're young. If you don't try, you'll never know."

This was a guy who was a successful businessman. He owned hotels, and I really respected him. I took what he told me on board, and that advice was one of the things that really helped me break out on my own and start my own business back in 1994. His words were incredibly valuable.

At a more advanced stage, I think it becomes harder to find the right mentors as you achieve more and more success. Quite often, you have to pay them, and pay them quite a lot, for their knowledge and their time and their experience and their wisdom.

Last summer, I was at a mentoring session with the legendary Jay Abraham, a very successful marketing and business strategist, whom I know you also interview in the book, Dan. He gave me some advice. I was struggling with a bit of confusion around some business partners and business strategy. When I talked it through with Jay, he helped me distil and find the solution to two big strategic issues. One solution transformed my partnerships with two of my closest business partners, which has had an enormous positive impact on our growth. My new understanding also strategically helped me drop certain things.

I was going in a certain direction with mentoring, but this experience actually helped me realise, basically, that the real opportunities were in two other fields. That helped us launch a residential property fund, which is going incredibly well. We've also branched off and launched another franchise, which has also gotten off to a phenomenal start.

Dan: *A similar question, which might get some different responses, has to do with your business journey. How have your problems changed? How have your challenges changed as you've grown in size?*

Steve: The problems have changed as we've grown. A friend of mine once said, "Steve, if you're in business, you will always have problems. The only really big problem is having a belief that you're never going to have any problems." That utopia does not exist. One day, or one week, or one month, sales and marketing will be broken. When you fix that, then finance will be broken, and then you fix that, and human resources is broken, and then you fix that and its operations. Once you fix that, you're back to sales and marketing.

If you're in business, you will always have problems. The only really big problem is having a belief that you're never going to have any problems.

There is always something in business. Things are very, very dynamic. And things are always broken. Starting out, it's about having a product and a service that actually works, and that people want to buy. It's about making those early sales and banking the cash so you're actually getting paid on time. As it gets bigger, it's about recruiting the right people, whether business partners or staff, always making sure you've got the right people on the bus.

As I grew the business, one of the next challenges was figuring out where I was going, if I was in the right business, the right industry, the right sector. That was a really tough one, actually, because I basically had to almost do a complete U-turn and give up everything I knew about a particular sector to go into real estate where I was a complete and utter novice. That's quite a major thing to realise you're actually in the wrong business or the wrong industry. That was certainly a painful transition but a really good one. I came out the other side very much stronger.

Another issue is getting staff and building teams. At one point, we were having real problems with recruiting the right people at more senior levels where the impact of getting it wrong is quite painful. If you employ a managing director (MD) and they don't work out, it's a lot of egg on your face and a lot of frustrated staff.

I think it's important to have that acceptance that business is not easy. It's amazing fun, and it can be really challenging and highly rewarding, but it's not easy. Don't go into it expecting it to be easy.

Concerning gazelles or potential gazelles, probably the number one thing that I get asked from fast growing businesses and very successful people is, "how do you get that key person on your team to help you scale? How do you find an MD that is aligned with your values and with whom you work well?" People quite often say, "Well, I tried that. I tried an MD or an ops director, I tried a business partner and it didn't work out."

Sadly I think a lot of people get really jaded from that experience, which leads them to say, "Been there, done that, got the t-shirt, didn't work for me. The only way I can grow is by keeping control of everything and I have to be the MD." All I can say is that it's almost impossible to become a gazelle and have sustainable, ongoing growth if you don't have the right members of senior team around.

When I was going through this challenge of scaling the business and wanted someone to be the MD who was much better at it than me, I talked to a good friend and mentor of mine, Simon Woodroffe, who founded YO! Sushi. I said, "Simon, what did you do?" He said, "Steve, I got to the point where I had five restaurants. They were going really, really well. But things then started to break and go out of control. The brand was amazing, but all the financial, the operational, and the human resource issues started happening and I basically promoted my ops director to my managing director. He dealt with the banks, he got the funding, he put all of the procedures and systems into place so I could be the figurehead of the business. He was the guy in the background. YO! Sushi's success is as much down to him as it is down to me."

So I took that on board and realised that, if you're a great manager, then maybe you are the right person to be the MD. But in our case, we've got 35 staff in one business, with about 70 across the group and another 60 working as part-time mentors, coaches, consultants. Out of all those people, not a single one reports to me. We often joke in my businesses that actually I report to my PA and that's kind of how it works. I'm a great leader, but I'm a really poor manager. So make sure you find people that are good at the things that you're not.

Dan: *What are you still working on in your business now?*

Steve: Right now, we're in a really big growth phase. We've got the solid foundation. We grew a few years ago and then a few things started breaking. We made some bad decisions that didn't work out, so we consolidated for about two and a half years. We put our solid platforms back into place; people, systems, structures, IT, all of that sort of stuff. That's done, and we're now in a very fast growth phase again.

As I said, we're launching a residential property fund looking to acquire another £10 million worth of property this year. We've just launched a new franchise business last week using our expertise and our competence. We've already got ten people signed up to that, with another 40 likely to sign up in the next ten days. That one's just absolutely flying.

And then the core business, Platinum Property Partners, is achieving solid, stable, steady, consistent, month on month growth. It's never going to set the world on fire in terms of growing 30, 40, 50 percent per annum. But it's slow, steady, and sustainable. It does what it says on the tin. We've got a very, very high degree of success with people, so that business is continuing in the background. These two other opportunities are really where we're going to capitalise on the foundations we've laid.

Dan: *What advice would you give to those who are looking to become a gazelle, i.e.: they're not a million in base revenue yet? And then what advice would you give to those that are looking to take their businesses to ten million and beyond?*

Steve: One piece of advice for both is just be clear about why you want to get to a million. Why do you want to become a gazelle, for example, or sail to the next level? That's a really important question and I always encourage people to be clear on their personal goals, their primary objectives, and the kind of life they want to create.

When I do a keynote, my main talk is called *Stand on the Shoulders of Giants*. One of the things I discuss is the sad reality that most people spend more time planning their summer holiday than they do the rest of their life. And so, when I lost everything and had to start again, I started with a blank sheet of paper. I put some goals, some principles, and some decisions down on that piece of paper.

One of those decisions was that I wanted to take one-week holiday every month, so essentially three months holiday a year. I had no idea how I was going to achieve it, but I enjoyed working and I didn't really want to stop. I can't ever see myself retiring. And honestly, what do people do when they retire? I think for most people, it's called the deferred life plan. They put life on hold and then wait until they're 60 or 65, when their bodies are failing and people around them are dying. That's when you're supposed to enjoy your life. I thought, no, I want to enjoy my life all the way through. So I set some goals personally.

Then I put down that I only wanted to work with people I like and trust. I didn't know how I was going to achieve that one. I didn't want to say no to paying customers, but actually, over time, I created businesses that served my personal objectives, so that's the first thing I would say. Make a list of some things that are really important to you, then work towards those and get the business to feed into them.

As part of that process, when you're thinking about the business, ask yourself if you're in the right industry. Are you in the right sector? Did you wander into it? Is it something you've just done? As I said, when I made a complete change, that was one of the hardest decisions, and it's especially difficult if you're making revenue doing what you're doing. But deep down, if you're not enjoying what you're doing or who you're doing it for or why you're doing it, then reassess. I think life is too short.

Steve Jobs said, "I have looked in the mirror every morning and asked myself: 'If today were the last day of my life, would I want to do what I am about to do today?' And whenever the answer has been "No" for too many days in a row, I know I need to change something." I have always lived that mantra, and I've taught it to others. Make sure you are enjoying what you do or moving yourself in that direction.

When it comes down to the growth and the numbers, I'm a great believer in adding maximum value. The franchise businesses we've got has broken records. Not because we're the cheapest. In fact, we're the most expensive. But we pride ourselves on being the best. If you have a relentless focus and dedication to your customer, you must look at what the competition are doing to really understand. Whenever I go into a new industry or new sector, I find out as much as I possibly can. I try to meet the founders or the directors of other businesses.

It's crucial to know the space you operate in. Understand other people's competitive advantage and develop a way of delivering your product or service and selling and marketing your product and service that is better than what anybody else does. That gives you that competitive advantage. It gives you that increased margin to scale and grow and develop.

CHAPTER 4

CRITICAL THINKING

"The problem is not the problem. The problem is
your attitude about the problem."

— CAPTAIN JACK SPARROW

Problem or Symptom?

"If somebody would just do X, then my problem will be solved."

That's how I used to think.

When I lost a fortune in my first business and racked up about £109,000 worth of personal debt, I thought, if somebody just gave me the money to pay this debt, the problem would be solved.

It wouldn't.

At best, it would put a sticking plaster over the problem temporarily and ultimately lead to worse results. Why? Because the problem will resurface unless you get to the root cause. The money is just a symptom.

Take a moment to think right now about the biggest problem in your business.

Now let me ask you a simple question. Is that the problem or is it just a symptom?

Is the lack of money in your bank account the problem? No, it's a symptom of poor thinking, poor planning, poor sales process, and poor profit margins.

Is that difficult employee the problem? No, she or he is a symptom of sloppy, careless, or non-existent hiring practices.

Is that lawsuit the problem? No, it's a symptom of something greater: you didn't upstream, you delivered poor customer service and antagonised the customer, your salesmen are too aggressive, or you don't have the right terms and conditions and contracts in place. The list goes on.

The problem is never the problem. The problem is that you don't know how to think about the problem. You have to first identify and fix the root cause.

I run into many business owners who think, "As soon as I settle this lawsuit" or "If only this lawsuit would go away, then I could get back to running my business." But the problem is never the problem. The problem is that you don't know how to think about the problem.

You have to identify and fix the root cause. In my experience, if you give a man a hammer, he tends to think everything is a nail. A business owner who becomes successful because he is a good marketer or a good salesperson thinks the way to solve all of his business problems is by doing more marketing or making more sales, but normally that is the strongest link in the chain.

It is the weakest link that causes the business to fail. The things you refuse to get involved with, that you insist somebody else do, are what cause your business to fail. You say that you're delegating, but you are not, you are abdicating. These are the things that bring you to a stop, and these are what need your full attention.

People refuse to pay attention to the financial numbers but are then surprised to find out their staff are stealing from them. People who hate selling are surprised when they invest a lot of money into a marketing campaign only to miss the target sales required. People who are all about creating high quality products or service, get clients or customers who love them, but are then surprised when they don't get enough leads in the door to make an ROI on the initial investment of creating the products.

The good news, however, is that once you can identify what is currently keeping your business stuck—the choke point restricting your profits, sucking your time dry, and giving you unneeded drama—you can release it, and the results can be exponentially larger.

You can stop wasting so much time, energy, and money on an ineffective strategy. If you are putting a lot of effort into something but 90 percent of that effort is being wasted, you can keep pushing harder, but you are going to burn out. It is about putting your energy in the right places and maximising your return on investment.

Let me give you a great example. When a client of mine, Sarah, comes to me, she has a very successful training company. She is doing about £400,000 worth of revenue. She wants to increase her revenue by 50 percent, to £600,000. I get the sense there must be a reason she is after that specific figure. People don't want growth for growth's sake. There is always an underlying motivation and, as was revealed in Sarah's case, it's usually emotional.

To get to her truth, I begin by asking why she is after that amount.

She says, "Well, I'm looking to grow and I want to dominate the marketplace."

That sounds like a surface answer. I dig and dig and dig, and eventually I say, "What's the motive behind it? What would it do for you?"

"I'll make more profit," Sarah tells me.

That might be true, but not always. More sales doesn't necessarily equal more profit. So I ask her, "What do you want the 'more profit' for?"

She breaks down and cries. "I'm worried that my husband is going to have a heart attack. He is working his butt off in a job that he hates, and I'm afraid if he keeps going, he's going to die."

I say, "What does your husband do?"

"He's a corporate lawyer."

"In that case," I say, "maybe he deserves to die."

(I didn't really say that - Only joking.)

What I said was, "Okay, so you're saying you want this revenue because you want your husband to quit his job, but how much does he make?"

"£60,000 a year."

"Is that gross or net?"

Sarah didn't know.

"Okay, I'm trying to solve this problem, but I need specifics." I tell her, "Don't you think it would be a good idea to first quantify the issue?"

She agreed, then came back and said, "£5,000 a month gross." We figured out after taxes that was £3,200 a month net.

"So what you're saying is you need to find a way of getting £3,200 a month more net take home, so that your husband can quit his job without pressure and without loss of lifestyle, allowing him to find something he loves to do?"

Sarah said, "That's right."

After analysing the financial numbers in the business (and I'll get into more specifics about how we did this in a later chapter), I found an immediate savings she could make in taxes. Not only could she make an immediate savings, but, in fact, she also had a significant rebate. When I spoke to her two weeks later, she shared that she had been able to get the desired result without significant impact to her business. An accountant I introduced her to showed her how to get an immediate £20,000 rebate, allowing her to take home more than enough extra each month from future tax savings and making it possible for her husband to quit his job right away.

Sarah was trying to solve the problem that "wasn't" rather than the problem that "was." She was able to transform the life of her husband and her children, purely with the power of critical thinking.

ACTION ITEMS

Immediately:

Take 30 minutes. Lock yourself in a room, turn your phone off, and answer these questions:

1. Generically, of your leverage points, write down which are your strongest and which are your weakest.

2. How can you improve that weak link?

3. What is the biggest problem or choke point holding your business back right now?

4. If that choke point is the effect, what is the root cause creating this problem in the first place?

5. What is the one change you can make that, if implemented, will prevent this problem from recurring in the future?

In 30 Days:

Schedule time in your diary, 30 days from now, to review the success of the resolution of this problem. If it's not had the desired effect, do some critical thinking. Did you really address the root cause?

Interview with Jay Abraham

One of my close friends and greatest mentors, Jay Abraham, has shared an incredible amount of wisdom throughout my journey. I've always been particularly impressed by his thoughts on 'sticking points' - the ways most companies get stuck and stalled and stagnate and suffocate so they can never become a gazelle. Even more important, Jay revealed in our recent discussion, his realisation that there are an enormous amount of seemingly successful businesses that are, what he calls, 'successfully stuck'. After reaching a certain point, they become complacent and comfortable, or they think they have taken the business as far as they can, less their 10 -15 percent of annual growth. Nothing could be further from the truth, however.

Dan: *Jay, can you say more about this idea of being 'successfully stuck'?*

Jay: The majority of high performance, capable companies out there unknowingly, unintentionally, and undeservedly limit and restrict the number of buyers they generate, the number of quality sources they can generate buyers from, the size of the sales these buyers make, the number of products and services the buyers are eager to buy each time they purchase, the number of purchases buyers make, the number of quality referrals they provide, and the utility value, or the complementary products and services that could be very meaningfully and lucratively monetised from these purchases. None of this is the company's fault, because they really didn't know any better. There's no shame in not knowing. What is shameful, however, is knowing how much more is possible from the effort, the time, the people, the money, the market, the capital and not doing anything about it. If you don't seize the opportunity to make your business work harder for you, then you work for it.

Dan: *One of the key messages I'm also trying to get across is the power of mentors. In your opinion, what is the value in having a mentor?*

> *In mentorship, I have discovered that helping others hold themselves to a higher level acts as an unimaginably powerful performance propellant.*

Jay: Mentorship is so compelling because high-level coaches take people to a place they aspire to reach by working with them to achieve their goal. Mentors have been there, done that, so they know what's possible and they don't allow an entrepreneur to set a goal that is not worthy of them, or that's beneath them. That is an underperformance. In mentorship, I have discovered that helping others hold themselves to a higher level acts as an unimaginably powerful performance propellant.

Dan: *Do you believe that the problems of a smaller-sized business are different than those of a bigger-sized business? And if so, how are they different? What are the sticking points or what are the solutions for companies that are ten million and beyond?*

Jay: Well, I think that the biggest single problem you find with the smaller businesses that constrain them and hold them to their low level performance is that they try to be everything.

And the one thing they're not being, in that case, is the strategist. They're most everything else – they're the technicians, they're the HR department, they're the quality control, they're the production, the supervisor, the buyer. They're lots of things, but they're not the strategist, number one.

Number two, I think the difference between a proprietor and a gazelle/entrepreneur, is that when they have a good year and make money, their default action is to buy themselves a new car, or take their family on vacation. The really committed ones, those strategically focused on growth, if they made another £100,000 this year, would put that money into talent. They would be constantly reinvesting in infrastructure or in human capital. Concurrently, one of the most tragic but very well-documented realities in most businesses that never grow is that they don't really reinvest in the growth and the development of their existing team. Research indicates that most small companies get about 20 percent of their performance capability, of the intellectual output of everything, from their people. It's not the team's fault. Rather, it's the owner's fault for not leveraging the most leverageable and no-cost, or very low cost, employees to be trained. These are things people just don't think about.

And if you're basically losing out to the competition and the market doesn't perceive the value or the difference between you, you've got to really figure out why.

- Why should a customer buy from you and not someone else?
- Why should they buy your solution and not an alternative solution? Or
- Why should they buy any of those solutions?

I don't think enough entrepreneurs really think about that.

It's also interesting to think about the four categories of buyers, which are all categories that can be monetised:

Category 1 – Unaware and uninterested buyer

Category 2 – Aware and uninterested buyer

Category 3 – Aware and interested buyer, but not decisive about who to buy from or what means of solution to buy

Category 4 – Aware and interested buyer, but has not yet decided on the actual provider

These categories are incredibly important to think about, since each one has a different set and subset of impact needs.

CHAPTER 5

POWER OF MASTERMIND

*"You will be the same person in five years as you are today
except for the people you meet and the books you read."*

- CHARLIE "TREMENDOUS" JONES

Somebody else has already solved your problem.

Whatever problem you have right now, it's nothing new. You are nothing special. Countless people have done it and solved it before you. And thinking that you are unique stands in the way of finding a resolution.

Nobody is an island. You can't do it all yourself. The speed of change in today's world is so radical. The key to success and staying ahead of the curve is, as I've mentioned previously, to be the dumbest person in the room. Learn from people who have already accomplished the things you want to accomplish. Learn from their successes and their mistakes so you don't have to pay the price of making the same mistakes yourself.

Napoleon Hill coined the phrase 'Mastermind Meeting' and invented the concept. Business leaders, high level entrepreneurs, and world leaders have been a part of masterminds for years. Surround yourself with high level people, causing them to raise their game, share latest distinctions, ideas, and technologies.

A Mastermind gives you speed to solution. If you have a network of people who has achieved what you want to achieve, you can get the same results in a much more radical time. If you have ten people who have operated in the same place, you can get ten times the lessons, ten times the experience, ten times the advantages. These are the distinctions that make all the difference in a tenth of the time.

If you are surrounding yourself with people who play the game at a higher level, you'll naturally raise your own level of play. If you want to be a better tennis player, play those who play at a standard above yourself. If you play with people weaker than you, it's going to drag your standard down. You'll get sloppy and you'll slack off. Instead, surround yourself with at least five people who push you to a new high standard.

Turning Game Over to Game On

Chris is a private mastermind client of mine. He is a property investor. When he joined, he had overstretched himself on a two million pound commercial property deal. Unfortunately, because he overstretched, he made big commitments and some of his finances fell through. If he didn't find £200,000 in less than two weeks, he was going to go out of business.

Here was a man with a successful company, with staff, a healthy client roster, and a seven-figure revenue, about to go bust because of one wrong move.

When he got this news, by pure coincidence, we were at the mastermind meeting and he took the call on the lunch break.

Because he understood the power of critical thinking and the power of mastermind, he shared the problem with the group and asked for advice. Two other people in the room had been through very similar situations, one of whom had been able to turn it around, and one who tried things that hadn't worked and paid the financial price.

Both were able to share suggestions on what to do and what not to do, which ultimately meant that Chris, within a week of getting that message, was able to find not one, but two different funding sources. That turned a potential game-over scenario into a non-issue. He ended up with a better deal and a lower interest rate than he would have gotten if the problem had never existed in the first place. Your biggest problems can be eliminated almost instantaneously if you know what to do and who to do it with. This is what a powerful network will do for you.

Asking The Right Questions Leads to Huge Profit

Joan was looking for growth. After going from £600,000 to £1.2 million in revenue, her company doubled in size over a couple of years. She wanted to go to the next level and grow her digital marketing agency. When she shared her plans for growth, however, another digital marketer in the mastermind program advised her that it was a terrible idea, and that she wasn't solving the real issue.

What she wanted was more profit, and she thought more growth would get her there. By asking her some questions and analysing her numbers, the mastermind group was able to identify savings she could make, which resulted in over a quarter of a million pounds in extra profit by reducing unnecessary expenses and less profitable product lines.

Neither of those results for Chris or Joan would have been possible if they had tried to solve it with their own thinking. It was having the speed to solution from other high achieving, fast-growing business owners who walked the path before them that made the difference. That's the power of mastermind.

ACTION ITEMS

Countless researchers have proven that the most reliable indicator of your personal income is the average of the ten people you spend the most time with; therefore, you need to be constantly reviewing and upgrading your circle of influence.

1. Make a list right now of the people you're spending time with.

2. Make a list of the people you WANT to spend more time with and become part of your peer group.

3. Over the next 30 days, consciously choose to spend less time with the people who have lesser influence. Instead, make an effort to reach out to the people you want to spend more time with and buy them dinner.

Interview with Daniel Priestley
The Importance of Assets to Your Business

Now that we've discussed the topic of mastermind, let's hear from another of my mentors, a man who has also successfully navigated the journey from potentially successful business to a full-fledged Gazelle, Daniel Priestley.

Dan: *Daniel, for those who don't know about you or your companies, could you give us a quick background? Who are you and how did you get where you are today?*

Daniel: My background has always been very entrepreneurial. I started my first company at twenty-one, after having good mentoring for two years. The business did a million dollars in revenue in its first year. By year three, we made over ten million dollars in sales, so it was a very fast growth business in my early twenties.

I had the experience at an early age of what it was like to be making over a million dollars a month worth of sales (some months), and in my mid-late 20s, I moved to London, in my mid-late twenties and set up a training business, which evolved into a business accelerator. We now have offices in Australia, Singapore, the UK, and the USA. Along the way, I wrote three books, which became best-selling business books. I've also become an advisor to small businesses, or an ambassador for entrepreneurship with KPMG. On the journey, I've also bought and sold companies, I've done acquisitions, and I've raised a lot of money for charity. I've crammed a lot in along the way.

Dan: *In many respects, you're the inspiration for this book. I've learned a huge amount from you. What have been some of your* *biggest mistakes, and what have you learned from them as you've had this rapid growth?*

Daniel: A lot of people had a low point in 2009 because of the global financial crisis. In the financial markets, it was felt in 2007 and 2008, but for the small business market, we felt it in 2009 when it became very difficult to sell anything. Everyone became extremely pessimistic and conservative, so the sales approach had to change. A lot of people had to rethink their business models. Personally, I had a pretty negative experience in the years leading up to 2009. I had been running a sales and marketing business that built the brands of others.

In 2009, when it became difficult to sell products, the people who spent hundreds of thousands of pounds building their brands and collecting thousands and thousands of raving fans decided they had other things to do. They opted to go home and work in their home territories and not work in the UK with me. At that point, I found myself with a team of fifteen people and nothing really to sell. I had to reinvent and rethink the whole business, but I also learned a valuable lesson: that the money and the deals revolve around key people of influence.

So it was around 2009 that I had the insight that, unless you're a key person of influence, your full time job is to become a key person of influence, because all the money and all the deals flow around key people of influence. As such, as soon as I lost the key people of influence I'd been working with, I also lost the money and the opportunities. At that point, I realised that it was important to acknowledge my own experience and my own journey and actually build myself as a key person of influence, and do the same for the people on my team, so that we really owned our own assets, owned our own products, and owned our own opportunities.

I had to reinvent and rethink the whole business, but I also learned a valuable lesson: that the money and the deals revolve around key people of influence.

Dan: *I know you're a huge fan of mentors. Across the years, what's the single best piece of advice you've received from a mentor, something that influenced you and influenced your journey?*

Daniel: I met a gentleman in 2009 named Darren Shirlaw, and I explained my frustrations to him and told him I was trying to find a new product. He said, "Actually, you need to be the one who develops the product and develops the brand for yourself." Then he summed it all up in one sentence, a really pivotal sentence that's just as powerful to me today: Income follows assets.

He basically said, "If you want to have rental income, you have to have a house. If you want to have dividend income, you need to own shares, and if you want to have business income you need business assets." He added, "For the past fifteen years, you've been a business asset broker. You've never owned the assets, you've only ever brokered other people's assets and developed other people's assets, so that's why you're in the predicament that you're in today. Income follows assets, so you need to either develop your own assets, acquire your own assets, or continue to broker other people's assets while acknowledging that, in these sorts of times, you're always going to get undercut." That was a really fascinating transitional point for me because it led me to define and understand business assets.

What are valuable business assets? Things like brands, like content methodologies, like owning your own products and creating a culture that people want to work and high-perform within. All these things became a little bit of an obsession for me as I worked to understand which asset produces what result, and I now live by the belief that, if anything is not happening in my business, it's because I'm asset deficient. If the culture's not right, in some way, I'm asset deficient. If the products aren't selling, in some way, we're missing an asset. If the business isn't running smoothly, I must be missing a systems asset.

I now look at the business as an ecosystem of assets, and any problem essentially is an asset deficiency.

Dan: *Let's explore assets a little more. Obviously, we're talking about products and content, but are there also things like marketing assets? Sales and marketing collateral? What about processes, systems for hiring people? Is that an asset? The people themselves, the members of the team, are they assets? How would you define the different types of assets?*

Daniel: I define an asset – and this is specific to business assets rather than houses and shares, gold and silver, etc.—by using a pretty simple test. If I got hit by a bus and the business got passed on to my partner, what would she find valuable? When she walks in on Monday morning and looks around at what she's inherited, which bits would she find valuable?

For example, if she looks on the computers and talks to the team and says, "Do we have a database?" And they say, "Yeah, we've got a database of a hundred thousand people." Okay, well that's pretty valuable. If she said, "How do we generate leads?" "Well actually, we've got a blog, and the blog attracts over ten thousand people a month, and a lot of those people end up registering their details, so we have a steady stream of leads." "Oh, okay. That's an asset. What about these books selling on Amazon? Do I need to change anything about those?" "No, you don't need to change those; they just sell every day of the week, and it doesn't really matter that Daniel's been hit by a bus, they'll keep selling." Those are assets.

If, on the other hand, she looked at the brochures and said, "Well, these brochures are all about Daniel Priestley, and there's no one else on there, so now that he's been hit by a bus, really they're of no use or no value to us anymore." That's not an asset. When it comes to human assets, I look at the asset based upon the ability to attract and retain a high performer. If you look at a business like Google, do they have the ability to attract and retain highly-talented coders and engineers? Yes they absolutely do, so they have what I call a culture asset, and the culture asset is the ability to find a top-level performer within thirty to sixty days. Therefore, the asset produces the result. There must be an underlying reason that people keep going to work at Google, so therefore they have a culture asset. I'm not necessarily looking at the particular individual as the asset. Rather, I'm looking at the fact that the individual shows up and that, if he left, someone else would show up.

Dan: *Tell me this: How have things changed for you as you've gone through the different stages of growth? Not only have you had multiple companies and gone through acquisition, but you've also got different offices on three different continents. How have the problems changed with your growth? Are they still the same problems but at an elevated level? I interviewed Ryan Deiss for this book, and he told me he feels the same problems reoccur, just at a higher level. I've spoken to other successful gazelle entrepreneurs, however, who said that, the problems just change with the different stages of growth. What has your experience been?*

Daniel: In my experience, there are very definite phases in which different problems emerge, so obviously the first problem that most businesses have is around their product. As a business owner, you need to ask:

- *Do I have a valuable offering?*
- *Is there something that the market really wants?*
- *Is it something that can be sold consistently to a particular type of person with a particular type of problem?*
- *Does this product or service actually solve that problem?*
- *Do people rave about it, do they love it, do they recommend it and refer it?*

Those are the first product problems that most businesses experience.

You eventually get to a point where you absolutely know you've got a good product, and you know that people recommend it and refer it. There's obviously innovation to be done to keep it fresh, but it no longer becomes a big problem. You tend to evolve pretty quickly into assembling a team: *Can I find the right people to deliver this? Can I find the right people to sell this?* You go from looking for customers to looking for your team, which means you go from a sales person to a recruiter pretty quickly. Then you think, *How do I create a scalable model of this? How could I be in multiple cities? How could I reach people who are not geographically close to me?* You go through the problem of creating things like brands and stories and content and videos, and essentially creating all of those elements that create a consistent experience regardless of location, so the problems, I find, do evolve. I suppose one of the big shifts is what I call P&L thinking versus balance sheet thinking.

Smaller businesses are almost always obsessed by P&L. Essentially, the question is, how do we sell more stuff and keep costs low? That tends to be the constant conversation with small businesses. As you get into bigger businesses, you shift to balance sheet thinking, which deals with the way to develop assets. *How do we add to our balance sheet in ways that produce a consistent result? Do we innovate the asset ourselves? Do we acquire the asset? Do we copy an unprotected asset?* Those tend to be the type of questions bigger companies are thinking about. It starts with P&L but, once that's solved, problems are related to developing assets.

Dan: A lot of the things you mentioned, like the cultural assets, aren't literally on the financial balance sheet. Do you try to find different ways of capitalising them, so you are actually demonstrating the value on the balance sheet, or is there another method?

Daniel: Unfortunately not, because the accounting system as we know it is based on the industrial revolution model of land, labour, capital, enterprise. So everything that's evolved from an accounting perspective is designed to understand the industrial revolution model of business. The reason you get companies with ridiculous multiples in the text base and in the new entrepreneur revolution is because the accounting system doesn't know how to look at these assets. You end up with these multiples that don't make sense. So for example, if you take a multiple of profit on WhatsApp, you would say that's a ridiculous acquisition by Facebook.

The multiple of profit – there's no asset there, they might have been able to capitalise maybe twenty to thirty million worth of assets onto their balance sheet, but they were bought for a billion, so that means that twenty to thirty million was industrial revolution style business, and the other billion was new economy assets. If you were to take Instagram, you'd see the same thing. You've only got thirteen people but it sold for a billion dollars, and that really comes down to the fact that you've got a young CEO, Mark Zuckerberg. He's inexperienced in the ways of the industrial revolution, building a business based on the assets of the future, not the assets of the past, and there's such a fundamental shift in business at the moment that the accounting system really doesn't have any way of capitalising those assets.

So, when I talk about assets, I'm really not talking from an accounting perspective. Here's a really basic example: a YouTube video that sits on YouTube for free and costs less than £2,000 to produce might get viewed ten thousand times a month. That ten thousand times a month produces leads, enquiries, and culture within the team because every new person who joins the team tends to watch it. It stops people from refunding because, after they purchase, they watch that video and they show that video to their business partner, and it makes them feel safe with their purchase. How do you capitalise that asset? Do you put it on the balance sheet as a two thousand pound production cost?

The traditional accounting method would probably say it's just the cost of production – video production would probably fit on the P & L—and yet it's probably one of the most valuable business assets that the company owns, but we don't have any way of recognising it as such. So that's an example of how we live in a new economy where we have to realise that the accounting system's going to take a while to catch up.

Dan: *You've gone through a lot of rapid growth over a sustained period of time, which is why I'm interviewing you as a gazelle. What are you still working on in your business today? What current challenges do you see, either in your own business, or in the wider marketplace?*

Daniel: One of the main things I'm working on is trying to capture insights. When you're in a business, you're getting this constant flow of insights. Unfortunately, when you're in a business, you often become so close to the operation that you overlook very valuable insights and take them for granted.

Someone who works with horses day in and day out for ten years doesn't realise how valuable their insights are around horses, and they don't realise that insight is probably incredibly valuable to a polo team or a horse racing team. Their insights are very valuable, but they're overlooking them because they're just too close. I'm the same.

Very few companies on the planet have the depth of insight into the entrepreneurial journey that we have, but because we're so close to it, it's so easy for us to take that for granted. A huge challenge for me is to get perspective on the insights, capture them, productise them, and add them to the overall experience that people have with us. The big challenge for me is maintaining perspective and seeing the insights for what they are.

Dan: What advice would you give to somebody in the early-six-figure revenue but looking to get to seven figures and beyond?

Daniel: The first piece of advice is that business is a lot more predictable than you'd think. The journey unfolds in a foreseeable way, the same way that every movie scene is very different until you're a script writer, until you're a producer of movies, until you get in the industry and you realise almost all movies are what we call three-act plays. They open with a problem or complication, they explore that problem or complication, and they resolve the problem or complication.

There are certain key attributes of what makes a good drama, a good comedy, and a good thriller, so this is a very well known formula. Movies evolve following a very certain pattern, and they almost fit within the exact same timeframes, but people think that every single movie is completely different. And yet, when you're in the movie industry, you realise that they follow much more of a formula than you'd think. Business is the same: business develops in a very, very predictable fashion, but only if you understand how it evolves. If you can anticipate what's happening next, you can anticipate the problem and find a very quick solution for it.

Here's an example: Right up until you have twelve to fifteen people on your team, you'll have a very flat structure. You'll have no rules, you'll consider yourselves a band of rebels taking on a big problem in the world, and you'll consider yourselves a lean, nimble, high-performing team. You'll have an experience in which you can pretty much take anyone off the street, train them in what you do, and, provided they're motivated and inspired by the company, they'll perform really, really well. Once you hit fifteen, twenty, twenty-five people, the company changes gear. It will have a natural desire to either go back to the flat structure or to professionalise and go up to fifty people, so there's a huge tension as it's literally pulled in different directions.

You have ten people on the team who really want to professionalise the company; they want to hire people with experience, based on training and credentials and university qualifications. Then you have ten to fifteen people on the team who say, "We've never had any of this structure you guys are talking about and we've always performed really well. We've always made profit. Why are you guys trying to make us something that we're not?"

So you end up with a company that rips itself apart with half the people trying to be a professional organisation and half the people trying to be a fun organisation or a flat organisation. It's quite a difficult situation when you're too big to be small and too small to be big. You go from making great profit to making no profit, to having no cash in the bank, to not having any capital to run the business. All of those things become incredibly predictable. When you know what's going to happen, you can just remove the emotion and move through it.

The advice for anyone going from six figures to seven or eight figures is that actually early seven figures works, but mid seven figures doesn't work. You'll probably lose money, and it's only when you get to upper seven figures or early eight figures that you'll once again have a great business. So it's worth figuring out whether you do want to be a gazelle. Do you actually want to go through the hell of scaling a business from two to ten million, or do you want to stick around at one and a half million, have a great lifestyle business, have fun, forget about growth, enjoy the flat team and flat structure, and make your impact in the world in other ways? Which desire do you want? Because there is a huge complication in the middle as you switch from P&L to balance sheet thinking.

My advice is that more is not better. Sometimes more is worse. Up until a team of twelve to fifteen people, having more people was a winning strategy. From fifteen to fifty people, more will probably actually add more stress. More revenue was probably better from five hundred grand to one and a half million. It may actually not be better from two million to five million. Up until a certain point, personally getting out there and selling and marketing is a good idea, but after a certain point, it's probably not the best use of your time. Up until a certain point, going through growth and innovation was a good idea; after a certain point, going through some acquisitions is a better idea.

So, some of the winning strategies become losing strategies, or at least less effective. My advice to anyone who wants to be a gazelle is to know what you're getting yourself into, talk to people who have made the journey, read books about scaling from one to ten million as opposed to the usual books that aren't relevant for that period, and just recognise that a lot of the journey may be very different from what you've experienced so far.

CHAPTER 6

DEAL FLOW

"When You Come to a Fork in the Road, Take It."

— YOGI BERRA

Let's say you are an investor in property. There is only one way to know if a two-bedroom house in the North East of England at £100,000 is a good deal. Comparison is key. If you've looked at a hundred other houses in that area with the same number of bedrooms, you will have a hundred reference points as to whether the price that you've been quoted is a good or a bad price. You have deal flow, which means you have a better way of assessing whether or not it's a good deal.

Ultimately, if you want to have a better life, you need to increase your number of options. If you only have two options in a particular situation, you have a dilemma. You have to increase the number and the quality of your options to get better results.

The same thing is true when hiring employees. For most small business owners, their hiring strategy is *I need a job doing, let's ask a few friends to get one or two enquiries.* The business owners speak to them, decide they sound okay, and give them the job. Or they place an ad on Monster.com, get three applications, and invite them all to an interview. One of them doesn't turn up and one of them turns up drunk, so they end up giving the third candidate the job by default. That's their amazing strategy for hiring employees. Shockingly, they're then surprised when the person turns out to be incompetent.

Compare that to having the discipline to write a really good, thorough job ad, or heaven forbid, paying more money and getting either a head hunter or having multiple agencies search for you, providing one hundred different CVs. From there, you actually go through and screen the CVs to find the ten best. You invite all ten people to the stage one interview. You interview all ten thoroughly, and then you choose the best three for a second stage interview. At that point, you have three high quality candidates out of one hundred that you are confident are best for the job, allowing you to select the one you want.

You want the decision to be difficult because you have so many high quality choices, but the reality is most business owners won't bother. They do not have the discipline, they follow fake ambition, and they're not prepared to do what it takes. They do not insist on getting deal flow for any significant decision in their business, and consequently, they get dismal results.

Let me give you an example. When David and I started working together, he was looking to sell his business consultancy. He'd been at it for a lot of years, and he was looking for something new. He went out to market and put it with a business program, and he got an early offer in from a competitor for half a million pounds. David was actually seriously thinking about taking the offer because he was done and wanted to move on. However, I insisted that he consider making it a multiple horse race.

As Daniel Priestley talks about in his book, *Oversubscribed: How to Get People Lining Up to Do Business with You*, price is dictated by supply and demand. There is only one business like his for sale—that's the supply—but the demand wasn't high. I said, "David, you need to get a wider range of options."

Ultimately, he was able to get three parties to the table. One of the parties dropped out early on, but the other two ended up in a bidding war because they both had huge, significant, competitive advantage to be gained from buying David's business. Their bids against each other ultimately drove the price up to almost £3 million.

In effect, David got over six times the valuation for a company he'd been considering selling for half a million, and this all happened in the time frame of months. If he had been impatient and said, "Get it done, get it done," if he hadn't been willing and disciplined enough to work for deal flow, ultimately he would have been more than £2 million worse off. That's the power of deal flow.

ACTION ITEMS

Right Now:

1. Write down the biggest problem or choke point currently holding you back. You can use the same problem you came up with in Chapter Five.

2. Analyse your current options. What are your current strategies for dealing with this problem? (You probably only have one or two, which is why you have the problem in the first place.)

3. Brainstorm at least three additional solutions. You must keep going until you have at least three viable approaches, any of which could solve your problem.

4. Rank your options in order of preference.

In 30 Days:

Schedule time in your diary, 30 days from now, to review the success of the resolution of this problem. If it's not had the desired effect, do some critical thinking. Did you really address the root cause of the issue?

CHAPTER 7

THE MULTIPLIER EFFECT

"The most powerful force in the universe
is compound interest."

— ALBERT EINSTEIN

The multiplier effect in business is a mixture of complex, overlapping processes. You have the process for marketing to generate the leads. You have the process of sales to convert those leads into paying customers. You have the process of delivery, to get your unique product into the hands of those, hopefully, loyal customers. And all of these things happen simultaneously to produce the output of your business.

I don't believe in 'get rich quick'. It does not exist in the sense that you can do the bare minimum and get a great result. However, I do believe in leverage, meaning that, if you can identify the leverage points in your business, you can get compounded results. The leverage points are the small, specific areas where slight adjustments can have a multiplying effect on the outcome. When you have several of these leverage points adjusted simultaneously, you get compounded geometric results.

The key is to first figure out the following:

1. Where are the weak links?
2. Where are the potential opportunities?
3. What are the differences that make the difference?

Whether or not somebody leaves the lights on in your office overnight isn't something that makes a difference, but the origin of your leads, the headlines on your ads, the supply that yields the right quality products in a more cost-effective way, these are things that, cumulatively, can have a geometric effect on your profitability.

You have to identify them. You have to measure them. Then you have to start kicking the can, making incremental improvements in each of these leverage points to have this accumulative multiplier effect.

One Key Strategic Partnership Can Make All The Difference

A great example of this is one of my mastermind members, Simon. When we first started working together, Simon was in full-time employment and running his business on the side. However, in a couple of years, he was able to quit his job and get the business up to half a million pounds in revenue.

After some careful, critical thinking, thorough preparation, and the power of mastermind, Simon made a few significant changes. He identified that one of the key choke points was his ability to get a high volume of leads and have access to not just the high volume but the right quality leads, as well as having the right infrastructure.

He didn't have enough staff, and he didn't have enough space. Simon figured out how to solve a lot of these problems in one go with the right strategic partnership with another company. This company gave him access to a large database of their customers to share in the revenue. They also struck a deal so he could use their infrastructure and their team to help get the results. In one 12-month period, Simon went from half a million in revenue to over five million pounds.

He got a multiplier effect by correctly identifying the choke points, enabling him to put a strategy into place. This meant that, for a small amount of time and money invested, he got geometric results in his revenues and on his bottom line.

ACTION ITEMS:

1. Identify the key leverage points in your business and where small tweaks in each of these areas would lead to a compounded increase in revenues and bottom line profitability. There may be other examples, but you could start with the 5 Cs:

   Crowd – How many people are exposed to your business?

   Capture – How do you quantify how many leads are captured?

   Conversion – How do you measure to see what percentage of those leads become paying customers?

   Cash – What is the cash value? How can you calculate the average invoice size (total revenue divided by the number of customers)?

   Continuity – What is the continuity rate? How often do people purchase? (This can be calculated by taking the number of sales and the number of invoices divided by the number of customers. If you have 200 invoices but only 100 customers, your average is two. Each customer on average buys two times in a given time period.)

Interview with Rob Moore
The Importance of Leverage

Rob Moore and I have known each other for many years. We both have a similar passion for reading and business in the sphere of gazelle companies. When I look at the epic growth of his company and of the various elements of his brand, I knew I had to interview him for the book. Rob has succeeded in accomplishing what most people only aspire to: creating wealth from one platform and using that leverage to move across to other platforms, business models, and in different industries.

Here's what he had to say:

Rob Moore: The thing that first got me categorized as a gazelle company was property. You can leverage property. You can leverage the banks to help you buy the property, you can leverage the tenants to pay the mortgage, and you can leverage estate agent to manage your property. If you do it properly, leverage is what gives you fast growth. When I was an artist in 2005, it was certainly what saved me from being in debt.

It was the first kind of leverage springboard; and once I had it, it provided me with the financial security and freedom I needed to be able to go and do what I love — which is teaching, training, and writing, amongst other things.

Next, I built an education business around my results in property, which is now the UK's largest property training company, Progressive Property. This education business got me to the next level in the gazelle company sphere. Information marketing and information based businesses allow you to leverage multiple assets and scale very quickly. You can get great reach with social media at low cost, all of which took me from making my first million before I turned 30.

Three or four years later, we reached the £10 million plus figure. That is a considerable amount of fast growth. Since 2006, our year-to-year growth has been 40%, of which I am proud because Microsoft reports its growth as 50% for the first ten years. Once Progressive became the biggest training company in the UK, I systemised it so I didn't have to be involved operationally. Then I was able to leverage that asset to free me up to work on other things.

The minute you create something - a product, a service, a business, you can leverage it to get increasingly faster growth and bigger scale.

Dan: What have been your biggest lessons or failures along the way?

Rob: There is no such thing as failure. I believe that most failure is feedback. It is a bit cliché in our world of business, but I still don't think most of the world knows this: you earn or you learn. You try stuff, some things stick, some things bomb. I've made many, what might be perceived to be, screw-ups in my business career. But actually there were great lessons to be learned. They were only screw-ups because I had an unrealistic expectation of what I wanted them to be.

The great thing in business is if you fail you get a lesson. Whereas if you're an employee, your failures are linked to how other people judge you. You fail in your work and you're in the disciplinary or you get fired. But when you fail in business you get to roll up your sleeves, get the lesson and do it better next time. You can iterate your way to success in business.

If I was to give you a little list, here is what I would say:

1. **Don't bite off more than you can chew.** I'm delusional about this one because I get bored really easily and I need to do new stuff that excites me and like most diehard entrepreneurs, I think I can do everything and be everywhere and do everything and take over the world. While this might be one of my biggest strengths because it allows me to achieve terrific results in different areas, it's also one of my biggest failings. If I had just done one thing for ten years instead of everything all at once, it's possible I might have become the Warren Buffett of property.

2. **You need good counsel, good advisors and good mentors.** I really believe in that. When I was in my early days and we were disrupting and growing fast, I didn't have the calibre of counsel as I do now. As a result, a couple of my partnerships did not work and they could have had I not taken on so many other partnerships at the same time. A proper advisor could have guided me through the pitfalls associated with taking on and maintaining partnerships and focusing only on the most important partnerships.

3. **Keep yourself busy**. You've got to be doing enough to keep yourself interested. I know that we're all looking for this leverage to create time freedom so we can sit on a beach and spend loads of time with our family and meditate. While I think it's important to be mindful of the present moment, there is also nothing more exciting in business than being busy and having stuff to do. There is a fine balance between staying busy and being so busy that you begin to drop things and let important details fall through the cracks.

4. **Maintain childlike enthusiasm**. I think naiveté is something that I've probably wrestled with in my life because when you're naïve, you're excited and you believe it is possible to take over the world. You need this childlike enthusiasm in business. As soon as that dies, your business dies. If you knew at the very beginning what would be involved in running a business, you probably wouldn't go into it, so naiveté is important.

Dan: You made reference about the importance of mentors. What's the single best piece of advice you've received from one of your mentors?

Rob: It depends on where you are at in your life. I got given a piece of advice by a mentor at one point that had I been in a different situation, that advice wouldn't have been relevant or made a difference. The advice was, *instead of trying something new next year, do what you did last year 20% better.*

At the time, I had one too many irons in the fire it was advice I'd never have given to myself because I'm not that kind of thinker. I like *more, more, more*. I say yes to everything and it was a great bit of advice for me at the time.

If you are like me and you do too much or you juggle one too many things, take something you've already done and have already proven is working well, and make it better. Invest in it, scale it and iterate it.

If you're not like me, then that's terrible advice.

Clear Vision

You've got to have a vision because when you have no purpose, you live someone else's purpose. When you have no vision, you live someone else's vision. When you don't know who you are, you're always looking at other people, pedestalizing them and wishing you were more like them.

The clearer the vision, the clearer the path, the less distracted you are by shiny objects; the more resistant and immune you are to haters, critics, and all the distractions, the more of a purpose you have. And if you don't have any haters, you're not big enough.

Dan: *There are two lines of thought I've noticed from the tremendously successful gazelles that I've interviewed for this book. One is with regards to obstacles. One line of thought is that it is always the same problems that come up time and again. Ryan Deiss said that the key to being a successful gazelle lies with making key hires. Whenever you reach that plateau in growth, it's time to make another key hire.*

Whereas Daniel Priestley said the challenges always change because what happens at one stage of growth in the business is completely different than what happens at the next stage of growth. A startup needs to get traction, but when you're of a certain size you need to Systemise and have people and processes otherwise you can't pass down the vision. What is your opinion? Is it the same problem just evolving at a higher rate or are there completely different problems? How have your problems and obstacles changed as your company has grown?

Rob: I think the same problem will manifest over and over if you haven't mastered that problem.

Some of the common things I hear, it's good to make a mistake but don't make the same mistake twice. (If you're reading in this book then insert a sarcastic tone in brackets.) We all make the same mistakes over and over and over and over because we are who we are. The things that create the biggest mistakes for you also create your biggest wins because they grow you the most. The business is a representation of its founder, you. But the gold is that this mistake may be the greatest thing that you do.

The things that create the biggest mistakes for you also create your biggest wins because they grow you the most.

My company has had such rapid growth because I work fast and I think fast. That's why we're gazelles; gazelles are fast. At the same time I make mistakes because I'm fast, and because I'm not thorough or diligent. If I become more thorough and diligent, I slow down. Therefore I'm not fast, therefore I'm not a gazelle. You've got to make sure that those mistakes don't break your business. You do this by surrounding yourself with a team that is strong in areas where you are weak and can negate your mistakes. My team is very thoughtful and methodical and systems- and process- based, for example because I am none of those things.

Dan: Now that you've been a gazelle for such a long period of time and you're still growing at an alarming rate, what are you still working on today?

Rob: We are still working on scaling globally with a localized and nationalized business. This has been a challenge. Progressive Property started in the UK, and it's not quite as easy a business to grow globally while still maintaining the company's ethics and values. Property is a very local business from one town or city to the next, you deal with different macro and micro economics, comparables, evaluations, different surveyors and banks and so on. That's why I expanded more into business, personal development and entrepreneurship, because I knew that could give the company more global reach.

The two things I am constantly working on is 1. Getting the education and knowledge that we're gifted and graced with in the first world. 2. Emotional mastery. I believe you can only grow in business when you grow as a person. How you manage and then master your own emotions, deal with challenging situations and experience growth is one of the biggest gifts you have from growing a business.

Dan: *For those that are either just starting out or they're six figures, they're early stage business. What single piece of advice would you give to those looking to grow rapidly and get to the seven figure level?*

Rob: I'm not good at single word answers, so there might be two or three here:

1. Marketing is the first thing that you've got to get good at in business. I didn't know that when I first started. When I embraced marketing in my company, that's when we really grew. In the short term, the best marketer wins. Marketing is what gets you in the door. You need to make sure you're telling everyone about what you do. You're shouting about it loud. The louder you shout the more fans and customers you create.

2. Embrace how much you really want to grow your business, because the louder you shout, the bigger your business will grow, but the more junk you bring with you along the way.

3. Leverage social media. The key is a mix of embracing marketing and combining it with social media. Get great at that first and then get perfect later. It's a race. Get out there quick, get feedback from your customers, improve, improve, improve.

Those are the three tips I'd probably give.

Dan: *You've achieved something that a very minute percentage of businesses accomplish: you've gotten beyond £10 million in annual revenue. What advice would you give to those that are, say, at seven figures but they're looking to get to eight figures and beyond?*

Rob: The key thing for going from seven to eight figures and beyond is getting out of your own way as the founder of the business. Anyone can run a seven-figure business. Now it's easy to run a low million pound turnover business with only yourself, your business partner maybe and less than a dozen staff.

But you are still the face of the business, the customers maybe still want you, the higher level ones especially. Maybe you still do all the speaking gigs and you still do all the staff meetings and the performance reviews. You still write a lot of the operations, you're on the front line. Now if you want to go to eight figures quick, which you can, you've got to get out of the way.

Even if you love it. Sometimes it's harder when you love it, but you have to decide, what do you love more: Being the front man of your business or money and scale and making a difference?

With that comes fears like, *they're going to mess it up. They can't do it as well as me. All my customers and my followers want me. What if they put my brand into danger or disrepute?* Every business owner and entrepreneur on the planet I've ever met (and I've got billionaires I've mentored) have experienced this.

You've got to embrace your own fears, doubts and concerns and grow through that and let go and lead. Leadership is about creating other leaders and getting out of the way so that your team can become better than you in different areas.

PART II

STRATEGY

CHAPTER 8

ROI

*"Our brains are either our greatest assets
or our greatest liabilities."*

— ROBERT KIYOSAKI

Business is an investment. In his book, *The Ultimate Blueprint for an Insanely Successful Business*, Keith J. Cunningham talks about turning assets into cash flow. Specifically, your job, as an owner, is to make an investment. You're either investing in stuff or you're investing in people. Whether you're investing in equipment, machinery, office space or people, the ultimate purpose is to drive sales.

The reason you're looking to drive sales is to get profit. There's no point in having stuff or people unless you can drive revenue. There's no point in getting revenue unless you can make it profitable, and there's no point in getting profits unless you are able to turn them into free cash that you can withdraw from the business or reinvest to make the business grow further.

Fundamentally, business is about your return on your investment at the top of the funnel. The key is to measure each process, each step in the cycle, and improve it. Fundamentally speaking, most business owners are completely oblivious. They don't even think about this stuff. They just look at the end of the day and say, "Oh, do I have profit? Do I have cash flow?" But they're not looking at how they got there, or at the causes and effects.

Once you have measured the process, there are only two ways to leverage a business and leverage the results that you are getting: one is people and the other is systems.

Regarding people, it's about getting the best bang for your buck. How do you get a team full of A-players? How do you get the right people on the bus, performing at their maximum level of output, not because you have to flog them, but because they want to, because they're motivated? In the next section, I'm going to show you exactly how to do that.

The other leverage option involves systems. How do you have systems and processes in place to produce better results consistently? There is a reason why 80 percent of small businesses fail in the first five years, but 75 percent of franchises are still in business after five years. It's because they have thorough, well-thought-out, documented systems that allow virtually anybody to maintain that business.

Ultimately, for you to get past seven figures and be sustainable and profitable, you need to address both people and systems and know how to leverage them. That's what the rest of this book is about.

ACTION ITEMS

Right Now:

1. Identify your assets and operating cash flow (OCF) number for the past 12 months - assets for service-based business is often best defined as about labour cost.

2. Divide OCF by your assets to give you your current ratio - this is the ratio you need to improve as you grow.

3. Identify where your business is weakest, systems or people? This is the low hanging fruit for leverage to improve the assets to OCF ratio.

In 30 Days:

Review the ratio to see if it is moving in the right direction.

CHAPTER 9

FINANCIAL ANALYSIS

"It's clearly a budget. It's got a lot of numbers in it."

— GEORGE W. BUSH

The phone rings. It is one of my private clients, Paul, calling from Dublin Airport.

He is frantic.

He is deeply in debt with his business, he is losing money, and he is about to miss his mortgage payment. He is worried that he is going to lose it all.

Sound familiar?

He felt overwhelmed because he didn't know what to do. First, I reassured him that it was going to be okay. The problem wasn't that bad and the world was not going to end.

First, we had to identify the root cause of Paul's problem. Remember, most business owners spend their time and energy solving the wrong problem, which will never yield the desired outcome. The cash flow issues were an effect, not the cause. The real issue was about him understanding how to drive clients into his business in a more profitable way. First,

Paul was investing too much in his clinic. He had too much in asset, and not enough in sales. Second, he was buying all of his equipment.

By using the skills you'll find in this chapter, rather than just pushing to make more sales, Paul was able to Analyse his situation and ultimately find a way to help his weight loss clinics. He realised he could invest less in the machinery to produce a higher level of sales; he could work with suppliers to operate at higher margins for products sold and, ultimately, how he could collect and improve the cash flow of his business so he could take more money home.

At the end of the day, Paul went from having a business that was losing money, to increasing his revenue by almost £2 million and over £400,000 net profit. All of this was born out of simply analysing the numbers, observing what was already occurring in his business, and using that information to make the right decisions and the necessary tweaks.

Now Paul is not even needed in his business. He spends time there when he wants and he is making more money than ever before. That is the power of financial analysis.

If you can't read the scoreboard...

"If you can't read the scoreboard, then you don't know the score, and if you don't know the score, then you can't tell the winners from the losers."

Warren Buffett said that, and it's true. How interested would you be in a sporting competition of your favourite team or competitor if you had no idea how they were doing against the other player/teams, if you didn't know if they had won or lost? It just doesn't make any sense!

And yet, that is how 85 percent of business owners choose to play the game of business.

As iconic business mind Keith J. Cunningham would say, business is an intellectual sport and the language of business is accounting.

Yet the overwhelming majority of business owners have no clue how to read the scoreboard in their business. So they will NEVER know if they are winning or losing. They just run around on the pitch all day, hoping that somehow the ball will end up in the net.

Stupid.

If you want a truly exceptional competitive advantage over the competition, all you've got to do is learn to read the scoreboard. Understand the language of business.

Most business owners never will. They abdicate responsibility to their bookkeeper or accountant.

And most business owners end up grossly overworked and even more underpaid.

Most business owners only look at their accounts once a year. Why? Because they are legally obligated to for tax purposes!

Clear management accounts are CRITICAL for your business' success. Why? Because the numbers tell the story of your business.

What does that mean?

If you looked at your profit and loss statement for the last 12 months, every single line item on that report is a reflection of an activity the business undertook.

Put more simply, every single action you took affected the bottom line of your business.

The numbers are the EFFECT. The activities are the CAUSE.

So the numbers are giving you the critical feedback you need as to whether or not your current business strategy is working.

Read that again. Let it sink in. What I just wrote is very important.

Think of those numbers as the cockpit of your company's aeroplane. They let you know how to navigate your journey as safely and as smoothly as possible.

The faster you are trying to fly your business (i.e. the more quickly you are trying to grow revenue/profits) the more instruments you need. Not only to get there more quickly, but to avoid a crash!

But what if you *want* go very, very fast, or to play in the big leagues?

Just think about the dials in the cockpit. There are, literally, walls of them; hence it takes an immense amount of training to be able to fly a plane safely.

It's exactly the same with your business. Don't be dumb, like I was. Stop yourself from making stupid mistakes that will cost you (that ARE costing you) lots of money.

When I first had the chance to work personally with Keith J. Cunningham in 2008, I gleefully shared my plans to grow my business in the next 12 months. I was out of my mind with excitement, and I was totally committed to making it all happen.

He took one look at my business plan and the matching numbers and laughed. He instantly pointed out several gaping holes that, if not filled, would almost certainly guarantee the plan's failure, if not failure of the total business.

How was he able to do that? Simple. He could read the story of my business as told by the numbers. And because he understood how to translate that language, he could interpret where the problems were and what to do about them.

The bottom line, I took his advice and crafted a much simpler, easier to implement plan. Sure enough, in the next 12 months, I doubled sales and trebled profits…with the same number of staff.

Greater results, with less effort.

That is what you call LEVERAGE!

If I could achieve only one thing with this book, I would want it to persuade you to pick up a copy of Keith's "Ultimate Blueprint for an Insanely Successful Business" from Amazon. (Awful title, yes, but a great book!)

But if you can't wait, here are some key takeaways:

1. There is a legitimate difference between tax accounts and management accounts. You need to understand both. Ultimately, management accounts allow you to manage your business more effectively (the clue is in the name!)…IF you can read them correctly.

2. There are three financial scorecards: a balance sheet, a profit and loss statement, and a statement of cash flow. All are interrelated. All are critical. You must be able to understand each one. (Would you want to try and drive a car understanding how the steering wheel worked but not the brakes, or if you could use the accelerator but not the clutch!?)

3. Most small businesses use cash accounting while every single company on the FTSE uses accrual accounting. It is impossible for cash accounting to give you the clarity and the optics you need to maximise your efforts and turn them into profit.

4. The aim of the game is to convert ASSETS into SALES, SALES into PROFIT, and PROFIT into FREE CASH FLOW!

5. Profit and cash are not synonymous …in fact, they aren't even related! Case in point, is it possible to have loads of cash despite a loss-making business? (Answer -YES, just think of the British government!) Is it possible to have a very profitable business and still go broke? (Again, the answer is YES. It happens every single day!)

If any of the above five key points don't make sense to you, visit DanBradbury.com. Consider it your very own pilot training guide.

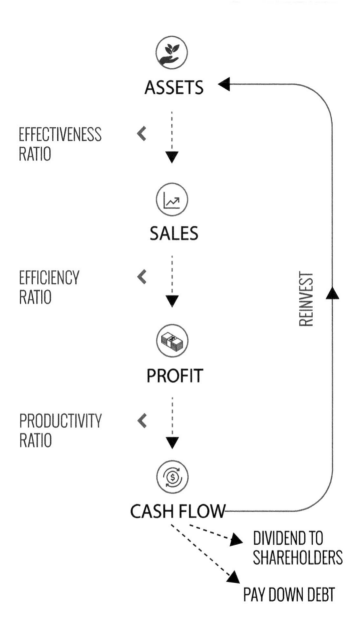

EFFECTIVENESS RATIO

ASSETS

SALES

EFFICIENCY RATIO

PROFIT

PRODUCTIVITY RATIO

CASH FLOW

REINVEST

DIVIDEND TO SHAREHOLDERS

PAY DOWN DEBT

Credit: Keith J. Cunningham - The Ultimate Blueprint for an Insanely Successful Business

CHAPTER 10

BUSINESS VALUE MAXIMISATION

"What you have to do and the way you have to do it is incredibly simple. Whether you are willing to do it is another matter."

— PETER DRUCKER

This one chapter could be easily worth tens of thousands of pounds in extra profit to you this year.

That's a big claim, but by the end of this chapter I think you'll agree with me. Here's why:

All business owners' desires can be fundamentally placed into just two categories;

1. **Money** - Most typically taking the form of free cash flow (FCF) from the operations, but fundamentally, it's a cash return for their investment, either as dividends or as a one-time capital appreciation, or exit.

2. **Time** - Whilst many owners enjoy working in their business, I've yet to meet one who didn't wish it was at least

less dependent on them. Whether they wish to spend time on higher value business development activity or they just want to go and play more golf, the common thread is leverage. More income for less time invested.

And yet, the sad thing is 94 percent are doomed for failure because they are looking for the answers in the wrong place!

Two fatal flaws are keeping them from what they really want:

Kiss of death 1 - "All I need is more leads"

There are few beliefs more insidious than this one. To believe that more leads will equal more sales, which will equal more profit, which will equal more FCF, which will mean more freedom for the owner, has led many on a long, dark road through the business wilderness. There are better and easier ways. (See below for details!)

Kiss of death 2 - "All I need is better (marketing/product/sales scripts/insert anything that the business is already very good at)"

Whilst I'm a fan of leveraging your strengths—or your Unique Ability, as Dan Sullivan calls it—the fact is, a business is a complicated machine, and it's only as strong as its weakest link.

Case in point; how many perfectly good businesses have you seen go bust over the years because of one thing going badly wrong?

Whether it be a legal, financial, personnel, marketing, or other issue, your business must be strong in all of these areas simultaneously to provide the maximum return for the shareholders.

Think of it like a football team. At a recent Success Mastermind meeting, one of our members was lamenting Manchester United's recent woes. "The problem," he complained, "is they just aren't scoring enough goals. If Alex Ferguson was manager on Saturday, we would have won that game."

I couldn't disagree more. At best, it'd have given some temporary respite. In order to have lasting success, you need to have a good attack, midfield AND defence. But that's not all. You need a depth of squad to compensate for injuries. You need a good youth academy to bring youngsters on. You need a club in good financial health so the manager can buy players he wants and not be forced to sell key players for financial reasons. In short, you need ALL the bases covered.

You're only as strong as your weakest link.

Most business owners have a tendency to focus on their strengths. After all, "that's what got me where I am now". But if you keep going to the gym and only do bench presses, you're going to get out of alignment, and sooner or later problems will develop. It's not IF it happens, it's WHEN.

You are only as strong as your weakest link.

And here's the great news. The weakest link is simultaneously your greatest opportunity for business value maximisation. It's the low hanging fruit to getting everything you can out of all you've got.

But to maximise the value, first you must define it.

How do you define your business value?

If you were to sell your company, at the most basic level, a broker would probably value it with the following equation:

Profit x Multiple = Value

He or she would take your previous year's profit and times it by a certain multiple from within a range for your industry. Let's say you own a beauty salon, where the multiple range is 2-4x. If your previous years' pretax profit was £100k, you'd be looking at a value of somewhere between £200k-£400k.

A Brief Guide to Business Value Maximisation

Step 1: Mitigate risks

The first question the owner from the above example should be asking is: How do I get a multiple closer to four, rather than two?

Well, investors are looking for reliable, predictable, and sustainable sources of income and will value them accordingly.

Said another way, your business' valuation will be adjusted upwards for growth and downwards for risk.

So, if you reduce the risk, your business' value will increase.

"But I'm not looking to sell the business!" I hear you cry. "I just want to make more money!"

And that's exactly why you need to reduce the damn risk! Nobody wants to make a load of profit for one month, or one quarter, or one year, only to get wiped out by some stupid scenario that could have easily been prevented upstream.

Increase the reliability, predictability, and sustainability of your profits and you'll make more money in the long term, whether you sell the business or not!

The first key to maximising business value is protecting what you already have. Remove the risks. In the words of the

Oracle of Omaha, "There are two rules to investing. Rule One: Don't lose money. Rule Two: Never forget rule one."

Look for the business' key risks and do what you can to mitigate them.

A mail order company I bought in 2007 offers a prime example. It generated leads online before sending direct mail to sell a distance learning qualification. Annual revenues were approximately £600k, with approximately a 25 percent net profit margin.

It was my first major business purchase and, unfortunately, I'd yet to learn the importance of mitigating the risks. All the leads came from Google PPC campaigns. The now infamous "Google Slap" occurred and, in less than 12 months, the business I'd paid over half a million for was dead.

Mitigate the damn risks!

Step 2: Reduce unnecessary expenses

This step isn't sexy, but it is grossly underestimated in its ability to improve your profits.

There are only two ways to increase your profits, to increase revenues and to decrease expenses. The low hanging fruit is cutting costs.

The problem is, most owners can't see the wood for the trees. One of my companies is a venture capitalist firm that specialises in business turnarounds. We were recently approached by a digital marketing agency based in the North West of England. They had approx. £1.2 million of revenue but were barely breaking even. They wanted £200,000 worth of funding so they could "invest in growth," with a business plan to produce £400,000 of EBIT the next year.

Having studied the accounts and met with the management team, we took a 50 percent stake in the company on a results-only basis. We're now three months in. The profit so far? £92,000. Our investment? £0. All we did was cut unnecessary expenses.

Is it possible to radically increase your profitability simply by saving a few costs? Well, if your annual revenue is £500k and your net margin is 15 percent, your profit is £75k and, therefore, you're spending £425k on various costs. Just a 10 percent reduction in costs would increase your profit by over 56 percent to £117.5k!

Step 3: Retention of existing clients

Younger entrepreneurs are always pushing for NEW. NEW leads, NEW ideas, NEW strategies, NEW products, NEW sales. But that's NOT where the low hanging fruit is!

In the words of the legendary Keith J. Cunningham, "How big would your business be if you'd kept every customer who ever tried you?"

Customer acquisition costs (CAC) are ever increasing in today's digital world. It's always more lucrative to retain an existing customer for future purchases than go out and put your nose to the grindstone to find a new one.

There is no point in throwing new customers into your business bucket if they then immediately leak out the bottom. That's simply a waste of money in terms of the advertising and marketing costs.

Remember, your business's return on investment is impacted not only by how cheaply a new customer can be acquired through good marketing, but also by how much that customer is ultimately worth to the company.

In fact, it's most advantageous to be able to spend more to acquire a new customer than the competition. Why? Because then you can completely dominate the available media to get new leads. One caveat, however: In order for this strategy to be affordable, your clients must be of higher value. And the only way to reach that higher value is to get them to spend more money with you, and more often! Hence, it is essential that you don't just become a marketing machine, but instead truly add value and turn your customers into raving fans.

But how do you do this? One powerful strategy is to carefully scrutinise the customer's experience. Whether through mystery shopping or some other method, look at the journey the customer goes on in order to make that first purchase from you? What do they see? What do they hear, what is the experience like for them?

It's not just about the product (although that is part) it's about how the experience makes them feel.

It's profoundly simple, but very, very powerful.

If the customer's experience from their first purchase is poor, they won't buy again. Too many business owners get caught up trying to look for the next magic pill that will flood them with sales. How about providing an absolutely world class first purchase experience?

Step 4: Increase Average Order Value (AOV)

If you owned a supermarket, which would be easier, getting someone to try your supermarket for the first time, getting them to spend more money when already there, or getting an existing customer to come back and purchase again?

The answer is getting them to spend more when already there! Why? Because they already know you exist, they already have a need for your product, and they trust you enough to be buying from you anyway, which means they have the means to pay! All you've got to do is entice them to either put more items in their shopping trolley, or the put in the same number of more expensive items.

One of my ecommerce businesses that sells DVDs tested a series of upsells after the initial purchase. The result? An increase in AOV of over 320 percent! The cost of making that additional revenue, approximately £120k in year one? £0.

Step 5: Increase Average Order Frequency (AOF)

After you've increased AOV from step four above, the next step is AOF. Why? Because you've already had the marketing costs attached when the customer trusted you enough to make the first purchase. Assuming the product/service was good, it's infinitely easier, and therefore more profitable, to get them to purchase from you again rather than go out and warm up cold leads from scratch.

Step 6: Ramp up the WOM!

Only once you've done the first five steps above would I try to acquire new customers. And even then, not all new customers are created equal.

In virtually every industry, one type of customer is proven to convert at a higher rate, have a higher AOV AND AOF, lower time to purchase, and a lower refund rate.

What are these customers and where do they come from? It's not social media, it's not direct mail, and it's not print advertising. In fact, it's not any type of paid marketing.

The best customers, on just about every metric you look at, are referrals from word of mouth.

So, what is your business currently doing to maximise the volume and calibre of your referrals? When was the last time you tested something in this area and tracked the results?

Most businesses are doing little to nothing by way of systemising or tracking referrals. This is one reason why most businesses will never become gazelles.

Think of it this way. You are spending money on paid advertising to get new leads, right? Well, since referrals are generally a much higher quality lead—a doubling in lead value would not be uncommon—if you neglect them, it's like burning money!

So, to keep that money where it belongs, it's imperative that you start tracking referrals. Whether it be in person at your shop, over the telephone, or via the internet, take the opportunity to ask how the customer found out about you. Ideally, once you obtain the referrer's name and contact information, you can follow up and acknowledge them for their referral, thus increasing the chances that they will do so again in the future.

However, even if you are just tracking how often new customers hear about you 'from friends and family,' this practice gets you started and gives you a baseline upon which you can build and see if your referral efforts are working. It also shows your staff that you are paying attention to this critical number and, consequently, makes them more likely to do the same.

So, how can you increase the number of referrals?

It's simple. Just ask! You can easily make it a natural part of the conversation, letting the customer know that your business thrives on referrals. Tell them that if they've had a great experience, you'd love to give that same experience to a friend, a family member, or a colleague.

The goal is to make it easy for people to give you referrals. You can even offer a free trial gift in return for the referral.

The key questions are when and how do you ask for referrals? Whilst it varies depending on the type of business, fundamentally speaking the more ways the better! Here are a few suggestions:

When:

1. At the point of purchase

2. At the point of delivery

3. A set period of time after purchase when the customer is likely to be feeling the most benefit from the purchase (e.g. one week after a new television is delivered, the TV still feels 'new' but they've had a week to enjoy it).

Other strategies my students have successfully used include at the point a client says 'no' (e.g. Even though our service might not be for you right now, can you think of anyone who would benefit from our service?)

How:

1. Face to face

2. Over the telephone

3. On the thank you page

4. In the confirmation email

5. In a letter packaged in with the product

One word of warning: I see a lot of business owners try to incentivise referrals by giving the referrer some kind of financial enticement. This is nearly always counter-productive. Often times, genuine referrers are less interested in themselves or more interested that the person they refer will have a great experience. And people who are only incentivised to refer for a monetary reward tend to give higher volumes of poorer quality leads. That is not what we want.

Ultimately, by putting some of the simple points listed above into action in your business, you can see your referrals soar!

To sum up, the above six steps are a brief guide as to how I look to maximise the value of any company I invest in.

Note, not one of them involved paying for Facebook leads! I'm not against paid media—far from it, since I actually do a lot of it—but I'm under no illusions. That's not where the low hanging fruit sits. Let's put first things first.

ACTION ITEMS:

The best thing you can do right now is take this book, lock yourself in a room with your key employees, and review the six steps above. If you do, this just might be the most profitable year you've ever had.

CHAPTER 11

DOUBLE YOUR SALES IN AN AFTERNOON

"Money is better than poverty, if only for financial reasons."
— WOODY ALLEN

I'm going to reveal the strategy that has added more to my business revenues and personal wealth than any other...and yet, I rarely talk about it.

If you are reading this book, you are probably like most business owners: stuck in a game you cannot win. You are stuck in the paradigm of trying to simply find more customers to buy the product you have. It's a limiting, uphill battle.

The most underutilised asset most business owners have is their customer list. If you have got a base of customers who trust you—because you provided a good experience for them the first time around—one of the easiest routes to radically increased profitability is offering them other products to buy. If, however, you have an amazing product, you just haven't got enough customers yet, the question is how can you got a lot of customers, all in one go?

What if I could tell you a way to do both, simultaneously? What if it could increase your sales by 50 percent, or even 500 percent, and with increased profit margins? What if you could do it in an afternoon? You probably wouldn't believe me. I know I wouldn't have, until I did it for the first time back in 2008. From this one strategy, I doubled revenue and trebled profits. I've executed this strategy half a dozen times since then, with similar results each time.

So what is this strategy? You acquire a company with a similar customer base and a complementary (not competing) product line. Now, before you immediately dismiss this out of hand as being 'too complex' or saying 'I don't have the money', let me tell you, you're mistaken. It's a lot easier—and cheaper—than you think. And it can catapult you to new heights...if you know what you're doing.

Firstly, let me tell you why you must consider this as a strategy, regardless of where your current business is today. It's got all the advantages of a good buy to let investment, but on steroids. Most people understand the concept of buy to let. You may even own one or more yourself. You buy a house. You rent it out and get an income stream that pays down the mortgage and leaves you with a bit of profit. Over time, the house (should) increase in value.

Here are six powerful reasons why buying companies are a much better (and easier) idea:

Powerful reason number one: You get lots of new customers instantly. It's up to seven times easier to get a happy customer who already trusts you to buy an additional product than it is to get someone to buy from you from the very first time. With this strategy, all the customers from your new company (company B) can be offered the products of company A, either as an explicit "these two companies are now one so we have additional great products to offer you" or, if the companies are kept as two separate entities, company B can simply endorse and refer people to company A as a joint venture promotion…just without any commission to pay!

Powerful reason number two: You get additional purchases from your existing customers. This is the reverse of reason one. Your existing company already has a bunch of happy satisfied customers, and now you've got an additional range of products and services (from company B) that perfectly compliment what they've already bought, only you have no R&D costs associated with the new products. You've simply bought them as part of company B and you are good to go!

Powerful reason number three: Risk reduction. One of the primary reasons small businesses fail is because the business owner didn't anticipate a risk. Whether it be the risk of a supplier, customer, or the business being dependent upon one employee, it's often about having a single point of failure which can unpack the whole business.

By having another company, you can reduce these risks by having additional products, customers, locations, employees and more. This is why, typically, larger companies have a higher 'multiple' than smaller companies, known as the P/E ratio on the stock market.

For example, Google has a multiple of twenty-nine. In other words, Google is valued at twenty-nine times its profit, whereas a small business may only be valued at three times its profit, or less. When you reduce the risk, you increase the likelihood of the business succeeding in the future and thus increase its value.

Powerful reason number four: Lowered cost base. This is normally termed as something like 'we anticipate cost efficiencies of £1.6 billion over the next three years' when you read an article on the BBC website about a large merger or acquisition by large firms. What they mean is, when you put two companies together, there are a lot of duplicated costs which can be saved. For smaller companies, this can be little things like no longer needing two separate accountants or particular insurance policies to much bigger items like only needing one office location, one marketing director, etc. Big or small, all these savings get added right back to the bottom line.

Powerful reason number five: You can borrow large amounts at low or no interest and flexible terms. Unlike buy to let property, where your options are greatly restricted, not only do you have much more potential upside with a company, but you typically will have much greater payment terms and flexibility as well. So, if you have a company with profit before tax of £200k and a multiple of three, the price you'd pay to acquire the company might be £600k. This would mean, even if you didn't increase the profit, you'd be at breakeven in three years but you'd have the £200k in profit on an ongoing basis and no debt. The question is, where are you going to find the £600k?

Well, normally there are three sources of funding:

1. Cash (yours)
2. Debt (borrowed money)
3. Warn out (Additional money paid to the seller only if some conditions are met. E.g. this year's sales figures).

What's most interesting is the amount of the purchase price allocated to these three sources varies widely. On top of that, in most small business sales, the seller of the company will finance a large portion of the deal. For example, a few years ago, I did the example above. I bought a company, complimentary to one I already owned, for £600k.

Its previous year's profit was £200k. I paid the owner a 5 percent deposit (£30k), and the balance was spread out over three years. I agreed to pay £570k to the owner, over thirty-six monthly instalments with no interest. In other words, it was designed so the monthly profit covered the payment on the £570k loan the former owner gave me to buy the business off him. No credit checks or references needed.

In reality, I was able to able to significantly improve the business, and consequently, I'd paid off all the debt in less than a year and I owned a business that made over £200k profit, that had virtually no dependence on me and zero debt. I later sold that business for a higher valuation and got much more of the cash up front. But that wasn't the best bit, which leads me to the final reason for using this strategy.

Powerful reason number six: Massive time leverage. Even though the company mentioned in the story above did make for a sensible investment in its own right, that was not the primary reason for the purchase. The reason I bought the company (company B) was because my existing complimentary company (company A) was highly profitable, but it had a problem. It really struggled to get enough fresh leads and new customers, but once it had them, it kept them for a long time and monetised them very well. (This is covered in reason one above.)

So, it solved the business's biggest problem, but not only that, it enabled company A to grow much more quickly than it could have done otherwise with any traditional marketing strategy. And that is priceless.

Clearly, there are so many advantages to buying a complimentary company to your own. Both companies can leverage each other for faster more profitable growth than is possible with virtually any other strategy. The key is to find suitable companies for a good price, allowing for an outrageously good return on investment.

CHAPTER 12

YOUR STRATEGIC PLAN

*"Everybody's got a game plan until
they get punched in the face."*

— MIKE TYSON

Fake Ambition

Ask any business owner if they want to make more money and grow their business, and they'll tell you yes.

Ask any business owner if they want to have more free time. They're going to say yes.

But just because everybody says it, it doesn't mean that they mean it.

It's fake ambition.

They're not really committed to doing what it takes to get the desired result any more than the average person. Everybody who is overweight and says that they want to lose weight, but very few people are actually committed to doing what it takes to get the weight off.

Now that you've applied the strategies of financial analysis and figured out how to maximise the value of your business, you must write it down or clarify it in a clear, strategic plan. Ultimately, this is another way of designating your key priorities. What major strategic objectives are you going to focus on for the next quarter? Not only do you need a strategic plan detailing which screws to turn, what objectives you're going after, and what obstacles you intend to overcome, but you also need to translate that plan into a budget.

You know that numbers are nothing but a reflection of the business activities taking place. So how will you measure that the strategic plan is on track? You are expecting this plan to produce a specific financial outcome. If you want to get a certain level of profit, you need to have a strong enough strategic plan, which, if successfully executed, you believe will give you this level of financial outputs.

Not only do you need to clearly analyse your top three priorities for the next quarter, but those priorities also need to have evidence of success. In other words, how will you know if you've hit that priority? If one of your priorities is increasing customer retention, how would you know if that has been achieved? Imagine your customer retention going from X to Y. If one of your strategic priorities is increasing the value, what's the evidence of success? Perhaps you define that as getting X many customers to go from spending £110 on average per purchase to spending £126.

In other words, you need to clearly outline how you'll know if you've hit it or not, and then, within each of these priorities, there might be a variety of specific sub projects designed to increase customer retention. For example, you might incorporate customer success stories. You might have an outbound calling program to check in on them. Whatever it might be, there are a variety of different sub projects that will help you achieve that strategic priority for the quarter, and, if those strategic priorities are hit, that will enable you to hit the financial results you want for the quarter.

In other words, not only do you need a strategic plan that clearly documents the major three priorities – no more, otherwise it's not a priority – but you'll also need to outline, in specific terms, how you'll know if you've accomplished those priorities. And what sub projects you intend to support the achievement of that priority.

In addition, you also need a budget, a financial forecast, to reinforce the plan. In other words, if you follow this plan, you know the numbers you're expecting. This will allow you to assess the plan's effectiveness, meaning it will give you feedback, or shorten the feedback loop, and allow you to adjust the plan.

Most business owners say, "Hey, I want to make all this money." They don't really have a plan, but even if they come up with something, it's not really that well-conceived. They just wait for year and say, "I didn't make any money."

You need to have a shorter feedback loop, which means you need to have a monthly budget highlighting what you're expecting to spend and what you're expecting to make. Every single month, you need to be able to compare what you forecast versus the actual. That gives you the feedback of the scores you've produced, which tells you whether you need to adjust the plan and if the plan is strong enough.

The most critical question for determining whether or not you have a strong, strategic plan is, "What's going to 'F' this up?"

I can't use this phrase because this is a Keith thing, but he calls it pre-mortem. In other words, imagine that it all went horribly wrong and it got completely screwed up. What caused it to go off track?

People come up with a plan and say, "Yeah, did you see the upside?" The reality is, you need to look for the risks and mitigate them. Just by burrowing your head in the sand, it doesn't mean that the risks cease to exist. You have to say, "I've come up with this plan. Now let me common sense check it. Let me bounce it off a few friends." Ask them, specifically, "What don't I see? What could go wrong with this? What could prevent this from happening? What could screw this up royally and prevent the business from getting the results that we want?"

If you're able to identify some problems, that tells you how you can strengthen the plan. Think about it from an investor perspective. If you were trying raise money in Dragon's Den, or Shark Tank, and you asked them to write a 100,000 pound cheque, they would be looking for the holes, indicators that the money is not safe. Look for the holes in your own strategic plan, plug those holes, and, ultimately, you're going to get a more robust plan. That effort will radically increase your chances of success.

Here's a good example of what I'm talking about: Alexis was running an online marketing company. He had a team of four people, but he was only breaking even, just scratching out enough money for him, his wife, and his son to live. He would have been making considerably more money if he had gone and got a job, but after sitting down with us and creating a thorough, strategic plan, he was able to critically analyse the right places to focus on, and what the financial plan and the budget would be. He asked, "What's going to screw this up?" and then planned accordingly.

Over the next nine months, Alexis went from just breaking even or slightly better, to over £20,000 a month net profit. That's a quarter of a million pounds a year bottom line profit. This was the same business as before; the only difference was a clearly documented, well-conceived strategic plan.

Here's what the strategic plan did for him:

1. It helped him clearly identity what the three most important areas (choke points, low hanging fruit) should be for the quarter. Prior to this, he was busy running around. When he finally took some time, sat down, and did a SWOT analysis, (strengths, weaknesses of the business, opportunities, and threats), he was able to clearly prioritise which three strategic objectives he could implement to produce the biggest results. (He used the Pareto principle to assess which 20 percent of activities he could focus on that would produce 80 percent of the result.)

2. Consequently, from the same resources and the same team size, he was able to get a much higher level of performance from a sales and profit perspective. He clearly thought through and identified the best investment of his time, money, and staff resources.

3. He created a budget to document and compare his progress, which allowed him to adjust the plan and keep the team on track.

Action Items:

1. Do a SWOT Analysis to help you clarify the biggest strategic issues.

2. Identify and prioritise the three biggest strategic objectives that you must make progress on in the next quarter.

3. Decide upon a budget that will enable you to determine whether or not the strategic plan is getting the financial results you want.

PART III

EXECUTION

CHAPTER 13

CULTURE

"Mediocrity knows nothing higher than itself, but talent instantly recognises talent."
— SIR ARTHUR CONAN DOYLE

Cut From The Same Cloth

For virtually all small businesses, people are the biggest cost, which, therefore, means they're also the biggest leverage point. A small tweak can get a much greater return. The question is, how do you hire the right staff or get a better performance out of your current staff?

Addressing that first part, let's talk about how you hire A-players. The definition of A-player, from a great book called *Topgrading: How To Hire, Coach and Keep A Players* by Brad and Geoff Smart, is the top 15 percent of performers in any pay grade. It's not about being able to pay more money. If you are paying people more money, it isn't a competitive advantage. If you're hiring people based on pay grade alone, you are more likely to lose them to another company willing to outspend you. The question you should really be asking yourself is, *how do you get the best possible performance on the money you invest in your people?* Clearly, if you pay more, you expect more out of that employee because you need to get a greater return.

So how do you get the highest performing people for the same amount of pounds?

A good friend of mine, Clate Mask, the CEO of Infusion-soft, took his company from a startup to over $100 million a year in annual revenues, with 700 employees and tens of thousands of small business customers around the world. I asked him, "Clate, if you could give a bit of advice to a CEO or managing director running a one million pound company, what would it be?"

He said, "It's quite simple. It would be to hire, train, and fire people based upon the vision of the company."

What does that mean?

"Vision has three parts," he explained. "Jim Collins talks about it in his book, *Beyond Entrepreneurship*: *Turning Your Business into an Enduring Great Company*. The first part is your business purpose. In other words, what's the lifeblood of the company? What's the reason you do what you do? The fact is, being a small business owner, there are going to be challenging times. What's going to pull you through it is the pure love of what you do, and you need to attract people to your company who are cut from the same cloth."

The Company Vision has three parts:

1. Purpose - the purpose is your why, the reason your business does what it does. (This never goes away - it's the company.)
2. Mission - The mission is the what, meaning what you are here to do. (This is your three to five year mission.)

3. Values - The core value is the how, the way you accomplish what you do. (This is a living, breathing document. The intent is not to have a document on the wall that no one ever looks at. It's a constant, ongoing conversation.)

Purpose

For me, the reason I get out of bed is to help other small business owners achieve their dreams. This is not a goal that will be achieved some day. It is eternal, so I want to make sure I'm recruiting people who are aligned to that same purpose. They know that this is the company they are coming into.

My company's purpose is:

We help small business owners to achieve their dreams

Mission

The mission, or as some people would call it, BHAG – Big Harry Audacious Goal.

What is the three to five year mission? What is your big objective? What's your big stretch goal?

The best example of a mission comes right back from 1963. John F. Kennedy said to the American people, "By the end of this decade, the United States will put a man on the moon and safely return him back to Earth." That was effectively the mission, the big massive goal that was a stretch for the institution that is NASA. It allowed everybody in the company, in that organisation, to rally behind that big, strategic objective.

My company's mission is:

To create the UK's leading small business success community.

What is that mission for you? What business vision can your company rally behind? It's not about making you more money as a business owner, because that doesn't inspire people. Are you trying to become the market leader? Are you trying to revolutionise the industry? Are you trying to save children's lives? What big goal are you after?

Core Values

I used to pay this idea lip service. I didn't really see its effect, since I was always interested in the bottom line. I thought it was airy-fairy stuff about "values," meaning how we behave. I didn't understand or appreciate how any of that affected my bottom line. That belief kept me stuck at around half a million in revenue for a couple of years. It was my weakest link because I wasn't getting people leverage.

What I came to realise is that nobody built a really great business without people. It is all about people. The fact is, people are the largest cost. So how do you get a better performance out of your people? The answer, is hiring people that are aligned with your core values. The more aligned, the more committed they will be, and the better they will perform.

Keith J. Cunningham's core values for his company are:
- Do the best you can
- Do the right thing
- Show people that you care

Think about it this way. If ever you have a problem with one of your employees, it is caused by them not behaving in line with the core values, and can be addressed from this perspec-

MISSION TO SATURN

CORE VALUES

- We engage & empower people
- We innovate & constantly improve
- We do what we say we'll do
- We say it like it is
- We are dynamic and decisive
- We invest in growth
- We face challenges with optimism
- We look for the fun in every situation
- We focus on the end result
- We make dreams a reality

MISSION

create the UK's leading
mall business success
munity with 6,000 active
members in 2017

PURPOSE

To help small
business owners
achieve their dreams

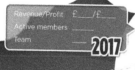

Revenue/Profit £____ /£____
Active members ____
Team ____ **2017**

SATURN MISSION

Revenue/Profit £____ /£____
ve members ____
m ____ **2016**

JUPITER MISSION

VITAL SIGNS
1. NPS
2. CLV:CAC
3. Continuity revenue (£)

STRENGTHS TO LEVERAGE
1. Live events
2. Relationship with Infusionsoft
3. Marketing strategy/tactics
4. Delight process

STRENGTHS TO DEVELOP
1. Lead gen/ Database size
2. Vision and Culture
3. Strategic future planning
4. Hiring A players

MARS MISSION

Revenue/Profit £____ /£____
Active members ____
Team ____ **2015**

Revenue/Profit £____ /£____
Active members ____
Team ____ **2014**

tive. When people are brought into the company, they know the standards by which you are committed to living when you are at your best.

It is not an idealistic, "One day, we will be there" philosophy. Rather, it is about creating the consistent standard for your business. If an employee screws up, it is the ultimate employee training program. What happened? Did you do the best you could? Did you do the right thing? And did you show people that you care?

If problems occur, they will fall in one of those three areas. As a business owner, you have to constantly call employees back to the core values, the code of conduct, if you will, of how they have committed themselves to living.

One of my company's key values is "We invest in growth," and that has a dual meaning. One, we invest in the growth of the company, and two, we invest in growth at an individual level. We are constantly investing in training. We believe that, to grow to the level and size we want, we need to develop our skills.

How do you practically apply this?

Clate says, "Hire, train, and fire to the values," and we take this seriously, letting candidates know in our job ad what we're about as a company. We're not just about doing A, B and C; we just don't want to market the person who attracts leads, captures those leads for a cost, and passes them on. Yes, we want that, and that might be part of the job description, but as a company, we're saying we're about helping small business owners achieve their dreams. We're about becoming the UK's leading small business success community and we list the values that we live by, one of which is investing in growth.

 We engage & empower people

 We innovate & constantly improve

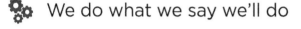 We do what we say we'll do

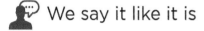 We say it like it is

We are dynamic and decisive

We invest in growth

We face challenges with optimism

We look for the fun in every situation

We focus on the end result

We make dreams a reality

In a job interview, you might ask questions like these:

- How have you invested in yourself in this last year?
- What books are you reading right now to develop yourself?

If somebody doesn't have good answers to those questions, they are not naturally inclined to invest in their own growth. And if they are not constantly looking to learn and improve, they are not going to fit into our company, which means they are not going to work for our company.

You need to find your own company values, which means you must define who you are and how you want your employees to show up. It ultimately comes back to this: if you are attracting people who understand the purpose of the company, are aligned to the purpose and the mission, have committed to the core values, and understand what the company is about, you can train competency. It's much harder to train culture fit.

What would you rather have, a technically competent pain in the rear who pisses off everybody else in the company, or somebody totally aligned to what you are about, where you are going and what you are doing, but perhaps needs a bit of skill development? You can give them job training and skill training much more easily than you can train core values. If they're aligned to the company, they will perform at a much higher level of output than anybody else. That's how you get your A-players.

Aligning Your People With the Company Vision

John ran a corporate event company, and that industry went through a tough time. Because his business was about having the right people to pull off corporate events, he aligned his company by crafting a vision. Not only did he craft the vision, but he got the employees engaged in a conversation of what they're about, their purpose, their mission, their big goals, and the values by which they are committed to living. By engaging them in the process, they became more committed to the cause and to the company because, ultimately, nobody comes to work wanting to do a crummy job. Everybody comes to work wanting to do a good job. The question is, as the business owner, have you empowered and engaged your employees enough to do it?

When John clarified his vision with his team, the transformation was dramatic. He made no structural changes to the company and no marketing changes. Nothing inherently changed other than the alignment of the people to the company vision, which resulted in an increase of 40 percent in his net profitability within 90 days. Aligning people to your culture can be that powerful.

ACTION ITEMS

Right Now:

1. Define Purpose, Mission, and Values.

2. Pull your team together and have a debate and a discussion about what the Purpose, Mission, and Values mean to them.

3. Using your team's feedback, refine the vision accordingly.

In 30 Days:

1. Review whether the company is conducting business in line with the Purpose, Mission, and Values.

CHAPTER **14**

METRICS

"What gets measured gets improved."

— PETER DRUCKER

Having good financials is critical because they are lagging indicators. Like a rearview mirror, profit and loss statements tell you what happened historically in your business. In addition to that rear view, you also need to see the future. You need to see the leading indicators. You need optics about what is coming. In other words, what critical drivers are going to produce the effects? If the financial reports reveal the effects of what happened in the previous month or the previous year in your business, what causes can you anticipate ahead of time as you move forward?

Think about this like a sales pipeline or conveyor belt. The lead or prospect enters the conveyor belt on the left and as they move from left to right a variety of activities happen to turn the lead into a paying customer by the end of the conveyor belt on the right.

There are only two areas we can measure to make this process more effective and thus deliver more sales. We can either put more leads onto the conveyor belt in the first place, or we can change the activities that take place on the conveyor belt to either turn more leads into paying customers, or convert them more quickly.

If we think about your sales pipeline, the things emerging in the bottom right corner are your sales. To make this process more effective, you must ask two key questions:

1. What do you need to put in the top of the pipeline?

2. How long does it take to get to the other end?

For example, if the typical length of time it takes a customer to nurture and buy is three months, you can predict what your sales are going to be in three months' time, depending on the number of leads you got this month. That number is a leading indicator as to what your sales will be in the future, once they've been through your full sales and marketing pipeline.

Sales is a lagging indicator—it's the end of the pipeline, the effect—but there are a total of five leading indicators that comprise the start of the pipeline, or the causes. At the risk of repeating myself, let me refer you once again to the Five Cs which I initially wrote about in Part I - The Overview of the Four Principles:

1. **Crowd**—A certain number of people need to be exposed to your marketing

2. **Capture Rate**—You can measure how many leads you've captured

3. **Conversion Rate**—Those leads convert to paying customers

4. **Cash Value**—how much money they spend on average, and

5. **Continuity Rate**—Frequency of purchase in a given time period.

They are leading indicators that you can quantify and measure that will give you the output, the effect called sales.

What does this mean at the execution of your strategic plan? The reason you have employees is to get a job done. Your contract might say you're paying them for 40 hours per week. You're not. You're paying them to perform a particular job and get a particular outcome.

Let me explain.

Every role within your company should have three metrics, no more, no less. I'm not a fan of job descriptions. I don't believe in them because what you want are standards to measure how well that job is being performed. That's the very definition of an A player. In other words, you can have a marketing manager, with a typical marketing manager's job description, something like, "Your job is to advertise on the social networks, driving people to our website to get leads for our sales team, who then phone them up and sell them the widgets." That's a job description, but it wouldn't tell you if you have an employee that you're paying £25,000 a year for that role. That job description doesn't reveal good performance versus bad performance, nor does it define an outstanding performance, so it can't tell you if you're an A-player.

Better than a job description would be a job scorecard, and a job scorecard might say, "We need you to generate in excess of 1000 leads per month." That's metric number one, the volume of leads generated, "at a cost of less than £2.50 per lead." That's a second metric. "Those leads need to convert at a rate of at least 10 percent. They need to buy our widget at £100."

With the above description, you have a way of keeping score so you can measure performance. You know whether or not the employee is an A-player.

Most business owners will never bother to have metrics for their job roles, which means they can never really assess performance. At the most, they're anecdotally saying, "Does this person do a good job or not?" And if you haven't quantified the notion of 'good,' how do you know the answer? Employers end up keeping people they like and firing people they dislike, rather than basing the decision upon actual performance of the job. This means that they often promote the wrong person, fire the wrong person, and don't reward or shape behaviour because they don't have the metrics in place or the standards to make it work.

Weekly Reporting

The key for this is weekly reporting. Every single week, employees have to report on their numbers in a company-wide meeting, where everybody discusses what they actually did against their three metrics for their scorecard. They'll have their actual results, as well as their projected for the following week. Then, the following week, they fill in the actual, allowing you to see what they said they were going to do compared with what they actually did. If they're doing a rubbish job, you can enquire as to why. "Is there a problem? Is the strategy not working? Is somebody else downstream not doing their job?"

This practice allows you to nip things in the bud before it gets to the end of the line and you say, "Oh my God, we've not made the revenues or the profits that we wanted." You can anticipate the outcome. Also, if somebody does a great job, it allows you to acknowledge them and reinforce and multiply the result so they feel even more empowered, and consistently perform at a higher level.

Ultimately, A-players like to be held accountable. Metrics allow you to hold them accountable in good and bad ways. You have a higher performing team.

Action Items:

1. List the job roles in your company.

2. Identify the three metrics to record for each role.

3. Define the standards of performance between minimum, good, and superb, and tie them to your team member's incentives.

CHAPTER 15

ONE THING

"How you do anything is how you do everything."

— T. HARV EKER

Every single action counts. What you're about to read in this chapter could be more powerful and transformative related to the amount of money you make next year than anything else you learn. Most people will tell you it's too simplistic and, because of that belief, they'll dismiss it out of hand.

Don't.

This could be the difference that transforms your financial future.

It comes from Gary Keller's Book *The One Thing: The Surprisingly Simple Truth Behind Extraordinary Results*. Nearly every single business owner that I meet is too busy. The key question is, busy doing what? How much time were you at the office last week? Were you working 40 hours, 50 hours, 60 hours, or more?

Answer this question honestly: how much of that time was truly productive, spent on the most important tasks, the highest leverage items that are going to actually make you money?

When I ask business owners this question, for more than 90 percent of them, the answers are less than four hours. The reality is, they spend most of their time on things that just aren't important. Most people agree with this concept, though fail spectacularly at implementing it. The strategy is very simple. Spend your time on the most valuable, most productive activities.

There are three parts:

1. Decide on your number one, most important goal for this month.

2. Decide on the first, most critical, biggest bang for your buck action you can take today to move you towards that goal.

3. Do that one thing first thing in the morning, before you get busy.

Brian Tracy covered it in his book, *Eat That Frog!* Mark Twain once said that, if the first thing you do each morning is to eat a live frog, you can go through the day with the satisfaction of knowing that is probably the worst thing that will happen to you all day. Your "frog" is your biggest, most important task, the one about which you are most likely to procrastinate if you don't take a new action or create conditions for success.

Everyone has the same number of hours in the day. It's not a question of having the time; it's a question of managing your priorities and putting the most important thing first.

Most people have a thousand excuses as to why they can't follow those three simple steps. Most people don't have what they want and will never achieve the success they desire. I don't think the connection between those two things is a coincidence.

The question is quite simple: *What's your one thing today?* Do you have the discipline to consistently clarify your most important project and decide on the most important step to move you toward your primary objective? Can you dedicate the time to doing that first thing each morning? This is the Pareto principle on steroids, intended to get the maximum results you want.

Deliberate Practice

Not surprisingly, there are many theories about the path to improvement. In his book, *Outliers*, Malcolm Gladwell popularises the concept of the 10,000 hour rule, meaning that people who spend the most time on an activity become the best at it. In my opinion, however, this is not strictly true. Otherwise, all people who have been driving cars for over forty years would be better than those who have driven for just five years. Continued improvement requires not just doing the activity but 'deliberate' practice. It requires the dedicated to push to the very limit of their skill set and to be constantly trying to improve.

Here are critical components of deliberate practice, summarised from a body of work on Deliberate Practice by Anders Ericsson:

1. **It's designed to improve performance.** "The essence of deliberate practice is continually stretching an individual just beyond his or her current abilities. That may sound obvious, but most of us don't do it in the activities we think of as practice."

2. **It's repeated a lot**. "High repetition is the most important difference between deliberate practice of a task and performing the task for real, when it counts."

3. **Feedback on results is continuously available.** "You may think that your rehearsal of a job interview was flawless, but your opinion isn't what counts."

4. **It's highly demanding mentally.** "Deliberate practice is, above all, an effort of focus and concentration. That is what makes it 'deliberate,' distinct from the mindless playing of scales or hitting of tennis balls that most people engage in."

5. **It's hard.** "Doing things we know how to do well is enjoyable, and that's exactly the opposite of what deliberate practice demands."

6. **It requires (good) goals.** "The best performers set goals that are not about the outcome but rather about the process of reaching the outcome."

ACTION

No surprise here:

1. Assess the work week that has just passed. How much of your time was truly productive, spent on the most important tasks, the highest leverage items that will actually make you money?

2. Decide on your number one, most important goal for this month.

3. Decide on the first, most critical, biggest-bang-for-your-buck action you can take today to move you towards that goal.

4. Do that one thing first thing in the morning, before you get busy.

You Have Everything You Need

"I hated every minute of training, but I said, 'Don't quit.
Suffer now and live the rest of your life as a champion."
— Muhammad Ali

In my previous book, 32X I explained how I took my first business from £100k in annual revenue to £3.2 million in just 22 months. But I never shared why.

My eldest daughter Summer was born with a birth defect called congenital diaphragmatic hernia (CDH), and required emergency surgery when she was born. One of her lungs had not developed properly and the prognosis was not good. Of the babies born with CDH approximately 1/3 die and 1/3 have other long term problems such as genetic disorders.

When she was born we lived in and out of the hospital for many months until she was well enough to come home.

Suddenly thrust into a situation where I had a much more important priority than running my business, I was torn. I still needed to pay the bills. I was a father now and I had a family to support.

And that's when I realised that until that point I'd just been messing around. I'd been playing at business rather than taking it seriously and giving it my all.

I knew a whole host of things that I 'should' be doing to make the business better, but I wasn't doing them.

I had so much potential, but I was letting myself down. Worse than that, I was letting my family down.

At that moment I made a decision, I owed it to my daughter to make every second count. Any time away from her hospital bed must be optimally spent, to add the most value it possibly can and ultimately give my family the rewards for my efforts.

And that's where this book came from, from tried and tested ways to rapidly grow and expand a company to heights that previously I'd only dreamed about.

And now you have it in your hands. These are the very best fast growth strategies I know of to take your company from where it is now to seven, eight or even nine figures. To become a gazelle company.

Like I said at the very beginning of this book, gazelles are the lifeblood of our economy. They create jobs and make a real difference in the world. This is your chance to take your vision and make it reality.

Your One Thing:

Now that you've read this book, the first thing you need to do is schedule time in your calendar to do the analysis required, come up with your strategic plan, and decide on your most important one thing. If it were up to me, it would be scheduling time to come up with the strategic plan for the next year.

Use the Business Value Maximisation Chapter to identify the low hanging fruit in your business. Follow this process, look at the six areas, and figure out how you can immediately see an increase in your profits in the next 30 days.

I told you at the start of this book that the biggest thing getting in the way of your success is your time scarcity. Chances are, if you don't do this one thing right now, you are going to be in the exact same position in your business a year from now.

You now know the skills and tools to elevate your thinking and take your company to £10 million of revenue and beyond, but the reality is that most people won't follow through. You will get caught up, decide you're too busy, and not implement the tools. If there is only one take away from this book, it would be to go, *right now*, and sit down, lock the door, turn off the phone, and schedule some critical thinking time to analyse your business. Do yourself a favour and spend an hour of your life to do this. You could probably do it in 20 minutes. Look at those six areas and weight it up:

Where is the obvious, low hanging fruit?

What's the one thing I can do towards making that tweak?

You now have everything you need to elevate your thinking beyond your current level and to take your company past 10 million in revenue. The only question is, are you going to do it? My experience says no. Use the tools in this book and keep yourself on track by going to **www.DanBradbury.com** and download some templates that will help you take your company to the next level.

Make it happen.

About
the Author

Dan Bradbury is an investor who specialises in taking companies already producing multiple six figures in revenue and accelerates their growth to over 10 million.

He is one of the finest and brightest marketing minds around, and one of the greatest authorities on becoming a self-made man. He started out with nothing and built himself up from the ground up. In his twenties he built and sold his first business for over £1Million. By 31, he turned around a company that was listed on the U.S. Stock Market for $4.3 Million. Dan has worked with over 8,000 business owners in over 69 different countries worldwide.

After a near-fatal cycling accident put him in a coma for more than a week, preventing him from running his own business for months, Dan realised that every business owner needs to have the same systems in place that allowed his company to manage itself in his absence. He has since committed to helping fellow business owners achieve their dreams with these strategies.

His clients walk away feeling he was the best return on investment they've ever made. They feel more enthused and clear about the direction of their business than they have in years.

Lightning Source UK Ltd.
Milton Keynes UK
UKHW021411030519
342067UK00005B/415/P